2/6

As one of the world's longest established
and best-known travel brands,
Thomas Cook are the experts in tr

For more than 135 year
guidebooks have unlocked the se
of destinations around the w
sharing with travellers a weal
experience and a passion for trav

**Rely on Thomas Cook as your
travelling companion on your next trip
and benefit from our unique heritage.**

Thomas Cook **traveller** guides

SOUTHEAST
AUSTRALIA
INCLUDING TASMANIA
Darroch Donald

Thomas
Cook

Your travelling companion since 1873

Written and updated by Darroch Donald
Original photography by Rebecca Robinson and Darroch Donald

Published by Thomas Cook Publishing
A division of Thomas Cook Tour Operations Limited.
Company registration no. 3772199 England
The Thomas Cook Business Park, Unit 9, Coningsby Road,
Peterborough PE3 8SB, United Kingdom
Email: books@thomascook.com, Tel: + 44 (0) 1733 416477
www.thomascookpublishing.com

Produced by Cambridge Publishing Management Limited
Burr Elm Court, Main Street, Caldecote CB23 7NU

ISBN: 978-1-84848-237-1

First edition © 2008 Thomas Cook Publishing
This second edition © 2010
Text © Thomas Cook Publishing
Maps © Thomas Cook Publishing/PCGraphics (UK) Limited

Series Editor: Maisie Fitzpatrick
Production/DTP: Steven Collins

Printed and bound in Italy by Printer Trento

Cover photography: © Superstock

Contents

Introduction

When it comes to reputation and tourism appeal, Australia has considerable expectations to meet. In the information age, saturated with mass marketing, it is not so much a destination as a brand. Think 'Australia' and instantly the sun is shining, you're on the beach or beside the Opera House, while the outback beckons and there are boomerangs or koalas... yet in reality it is so much more than that – and as much in size, as in content.

At over 7.5 million sq km (almost 3 million sq miles), the great island continent (as it is often referred to) is about the same size as the USA and about 32 times the size of the UK. In Australia, size matters. Skies are not just big here, they are oceanic.

So, when faced with this great behemoth and a shortage of time, where do you begin?

With Sydney as the likely arrival point, you are off to a great start. This gatekeeper to the nation is all that you might expect and little needs to be said. It is intense and stunning. Suffice to say it will be hard to extricate yourself from Sydney's powerful spell. After Sydney, the vast majority head north, and why wouldn't you? There is no denying the attraction of New South Wales' north coast or Queensland's reef. However, by staying in Southeast Australia you have decided to be different, to part from the migrating flock and head south. Wise move.

New South Wales' south coast is not a poor cousin to the north, but a rich one. Here in this little corner of the state you have more national parks than anywhere else in Australia. Among them is Kosciuszko, home to the mountain of the same name, which is the nation's highest and, yes, it's even covered in snow!

Only a short distance away is Canberra, the nation's much maligned capital, singing away quietly like a handsome caged bird trapped within its tiny state boundary.

Victoria? A compact state and the most populated, yet diverse in both landscape and culture. Its capital, Melbourne, is not as pretty as Sydney but it is just as attractive in other ways – cosmopolitan, happening and friendly, 'four seasons in one day', and proud of it. Surrounding Melbourne and within easy reach of it are some aesthetic gems like the Mornington Peninsula or 'The Prom' (Wilson's Promontory), the southernmost tip of

Australia. Then there is the Great Ocean Road, one of the most celebrated coastal scenic drives in the world, home to a few 'Apostles' and 'Winki Pop', a great break for 'the board'. From there you may choose to cross the border into South Australia and Adelaide, the most English of Australia's cities, laid-back, gracious and the perfect base from which to go wine tasting, or a stepping stone for some real adventure and an appointment 'outback' with Wilpena Pound.

However, we had better stop there because it has happened again. What about Tasmania? Poor Tasmania; perhaps because it is a small island it is the country's most forgotten state, yet without doubt it is one of the most beautiful. Like the Opera House, the Sydney Harbour Bridge or those Apostles, it is bigger, has more of an impact, and is more beautiful in three dimensions than you could have imagined.

The Angel installation, Melbourne

So you have chosen wisely and if you make the effort and the journey, one thing is for sure – you will not be disappointed. Hold a koala, dance with an Aboriginal or raft down the Franklin in Tasmania, and you will never be quite the same again.

Arthur River on Tasmania's northwest coast

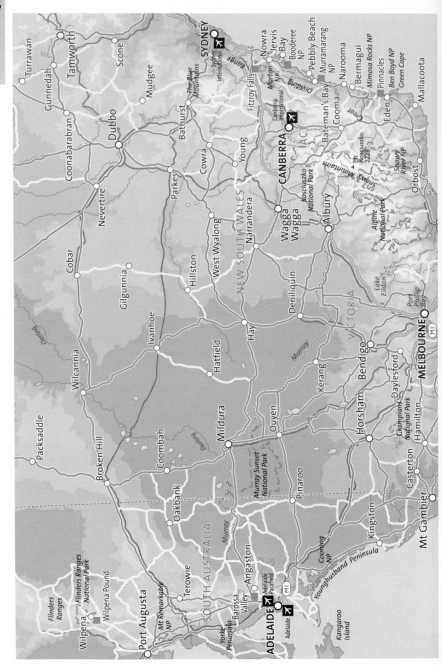

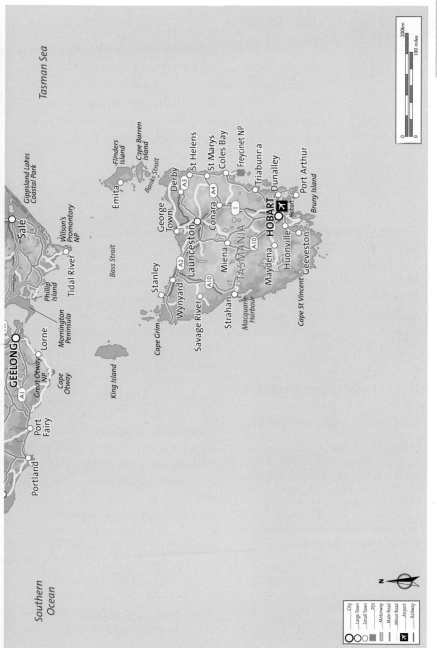

Southern
Ocean

Tasman Sea

Portland

Port
Fairy

GEELONG

Lorne

Great Otway
NP

Cape
Otway

Sale

Gippsland Lakes
Coastal Park

Wilson's
Promontory
NP

Phillip
Island

Mornington
Peninsula

Tidal River

Bass Strait

King Island

Flinders
Island

Emita

Cape Barren
Island

Banks Strait

Cape Grim

Stanley

Wynyard

Savage River

Strahan

Macquarie
Harbour

George
Town

Derby

A3

St Helens

St Marys

A4

Coles Bay

Freycinet NP

Launceston

Conara

Triabunna

Dunalley

Port Arthur

Miena

Maydena

TASMANIA

A2

A10

A10

1

Huonville

Geeveston

HOBART

Hobart

Cape St Vincent

Bruny Island

N

City
Large Town
Small Town
POI
Motorway
Main Road
Minor Road
Airport
Railway

200km

100 miles

The land

At over 7.5 million sq km (almost 3 million sq miles), Australia accounts for 5 per cent of the world's land area and is its sixth-largest country. There are 22 million people living in Australia (the USA has 300 million), and not surprisingly – being one of the driest places on earth – the vast majority live along the coastal fringes.

The long and the short of it

The coastal fringes of the eastern states of Queensland, New South Wales and Victoria have by far the highest population densities. This is due in no small part to the Great Dividing Range, which adds that vital equivalent of a geological rain dance. The majority

CAPTAIN JAMES COOK

Captain James Cook (1728–79) was an extraordinary man from humble beginnings and is widely regarded as the greatest explorer of all time. He was born in Yorkshire, England, and, after joining the Royal Navy in his teens, became known for his exceptional skills at navigation and cartography. In 1766 he was hired by the Royal Society of London to observe the transit of Venus across the sun. These precise measurements were necessary to determine longitude and create accurate maps. Cook sailed from England in 1768 and made his observations of the transit off Tahiti in April 1769 and mapped the entire coastline of New Zealand before landing at Botany Bay on the east coast of Australia on 19 April 1770; he was the first recorded European to do so. The rest, as they say, is history.

of people live in Greater Sydney (4.5 million), or Melbourne (3.8 million).

The Great Dividing Range, formed over 90 million years ago when New Zealand made its break for geological independence, is an extensive yet relatively narrow range that stretches over 4,000km (2,500 miles) from the far north of Queensland to Tasmania. It is also home to the nation's highest peaks, with the highest, Mount Kosciuszko (2,228m/7,310ft), one of only a few in southern New South Wales and northeastern Victoria that can make a brief appointment with snow in winter.

Australia's two longest rivers, the Murray and the Darling, are sourced from the Great Dividing Range and, these days very depleted, they join and reach the sea along the south coast in South Australia. The vast Murray Darling Basin is often labelled the food bowl of Australia, but now, since suffering chronic drought conditions in

2006–7, it has become the hot topic of social and political debate surrounding climate change and agricultural sustainability.

Diversity and climate

Despite the classic perception of an endless expanse of 'outback' baking under oceanic blue skies, Australia possesses an astonishingly diverse geography and biodiversity. This is particularly apparent in Tasmania and on the east coast due to the influence of the Great Dividing Range and climatic changes caused by latitude. In Sydney, halfway up the coast of New South Wales, a temperate climate with mild winters allows a hint of seasonal change, and subsequent habitats that result in a rich abundance of wildlife, even in the city itself. For the human species, Sydney offers the perfect climate, with over 300 sunny days a year and temperatures that rarely drop below freezing. In contrast, Melbourne, 1,000km (620 miles) to the south, has a 'four seasons in one day' label. Though it does not fall below freezing, winters can be both cold and wet. Moreover, in summer, depending on wind direction, a drop in temperature from the forties to the teens (°C) (hundreds to the fifties °F) in a matter of hours is not uncommon.

The land

A wave crashes ashore at Wineglass Bay, Freycinet National Park

Australian wildlife

Wildlife is very much part of the Australian holiday experience. Living icons like the koala and kangaroo are as much ingrained in our psyche as the Opera House or Uluru. The great island nation is blessed with one of the richest biodiversities on earth.

A volume of species reads like a who's who of the well known, the utterly spectacular and the 'you've got to be joking'. Best of all, you do not have to venture far to experience it. Indeed, it happens almost by default. Be it a flock of cockatoos over the motorway in Sydney or dolphins surfing beneath the waves in Byron Bay, your encounters will be many and varied and you will inevitably have your own tales to tell.

The icons

The koala (drop the word bear – it's a misnomer) is considered the epitome of all that is cute and cuddly. Koalas eat only eucalyptus leaves and have evolved to fill that very specialist niche. Of course, eating leaves does not require much brainpower, hence they have brains about the size of a walnut and move very slowly. Eucalyptus leaves take a long time to digest, too, which is why koalas could sleep for Australia!

Kangaroos replace the cute and cuddly with brilliance and novelty in design. All roos (except the tree kangaroo) are perfectly adapted for speed. They have evolved to conserve a remarkable amount of energy in motion, with their thick tails acting as a counterbalance.

Both koalas and eastern grey kangaroos are common on the East Coast and there are many excellent zoos and native wildlife sanctuaries where you can get up close and personal with them. Most have displays where you can hold a koala and get the obligatory picture taken.

The beautiful and the bizarre

In their wildest imaginings, Peter Jackson, Damien Hirst and Charles

Koalas spend a lot of time sleeping

The mighty Australian 'Saltie' (saltwater crocodile), common in northern Queensland

Darwin still could not have come up with some of the most bizarre Australian species. Who on earth, for example, can look at a platypus without dropping their jaw, or watch a roo hop without tilting their head and thinking, how come? Then there is the Great Barrier Reef, home of the 'Old Wife', the 'Bucket Mouth' and the 'Stone Fish', surely the ugliest face on the planet. And to top that, few people are aware that the reef itself is a living thing, the biggest on the planet, and that it reproduces on just one night every year, around the full moon, in one mass, spectacular orgasm.

And the nasties?

There are many dangerous species in Australia, and some can kill. The large, venomous Taipan (snake), for example, could take out a small household, and shark attacks do occur. But the simple fact of the matter is that the vast majority have absolutely no desire to make your acquaintance, and with a modicum of common sense, you will not be bitten, mauled, or carried off into the sunset shouting 'Croikey'!

History

60,000– 40,000 BC Long before European settlers arrive, and for many thousands of years, Aboriginals demonstrate an ideal model of a sustainable existence in harmony with the environment.

AD 1770 On his great voyage of discovery, James Cook (not yet 'Captain') makes landfall, naming the location Botany Bay. Continuing north he suffers a disastrous encounter with the Great Barrier Reef, running aground near what was aptly named Cape Tribulation.

1786 To ease a burgeoning prison population, King George III of England decides the potential 'new lands' would make a fine penal colony.

1788 The 'First Fleet', comprising six vessels carrying about 300 crew and 800 convicts, sails in to Botany Bay under the command of Captain Arthur Phillip. After an amicable encounter with Aboriginals, Phillip finds suitable anchorage and names Sydney Cove after the British secretary of state, Viscount Sydney. Phillip himself is quickly sworn in as the first governor of the newly proclaimed state of New South Wales (NSW).

1779–90 Initial attempts at settlement prove disastrous. The crew is ill prepared, poorly supplied and unskilled in utilising any local resources.

1790–1810 Sydney develops and grows with the arrival of more convicts and the parole of others. Phillip departs, leaving soldiers in charge of the convicts. The soldiers grant each other rights to secure tracts of land and use convict labour for its development. In the absence of money, rum becomes the currency of choice. Chaos ensues. England's first attempt to restore official order in the form of Captain Bligh (from *Mutiny on the Bounty* fame) fails, and it takes the Scotsman and new governor Lachlan

Macquarie to finally restore order.

1803 In fear of French and Dutch claims, Great Britain continues pre-emptive colonial action, including the establishment of a penal colony at Port Arthur in Van Diemen's Land (Tasmania). Van Diemen's Land was the name first bestowed upon it by Dutch explorer Abel Tasman in 1642.

1830–40 Victoria's first settlement is established at Portland. Melbourne is founded by farmer and businessman John Batman (originally born in Parramatta, NSW). The last remaining 135 Tasmanian Aboriginals (from a population of around 4,000) are sent to Flinders Island 'for their own protection'.

1850 New farms and settlements are established apace. Wool and wheat production in particular forms a solid base economy. Explorers William Lawson, Gregory Blaxland and William Charles Wentworth find a way through the seemingly impenetrable Blue Mountains in NSW, opening up the west of the state to settlement.

1851 The discovery of gold near Bathurst, west of the Blue Mountains, almost doubles the population of Sydney within a single decade to around 100,000.

1856 Van Diemen's Land is renamed Tasmania in an attempt to shake off its convict image.

1860–1900 Settlement continues in earnest and is largely successful, but the problems of racial disharmony and the sad disintegration of the Aboriginals and their culture remain a major national problem.

1876 Tasmania's last full-blooded Aboriginal, Truganini, dies, with most of her relatives already abused and murdered by colonials.

1877 The last penal settlement in Tasmania at Port Arthur is finally closed.

1901 Federation and the creation of the Commonwealth of Australia.

1927–50 Canberra, the nation's new capital, is established. The Depression and World War II come and go and immigration increases rapidly. Sydney Harbour Bridge is completed in 1932. With the discovery of the aqualung, the great 'barrier' of the Barrier Reef is overcome.

1950–70 The infant nation struggles to find its own identity and disenfranchise itself from its colonial past. Aboriginals are granted the vote and are included in census figures. Melbourne hosts the 1956 Olympic Games.

1973 With the completion of the Opera House, Sydney is well on course to becoming one of the best-loved and most dynamic cities in the world.

1988 Sydney celebrates its bicentennial in the shadow of Aboriginal protest.

1995 A federal enquiry into what became known as the 'Stolen Generations' (the removal of Aboriginal children to become wards of the state between 1869 and 1969) branded the policies as genocide and called for an official apology and compensation for the Aboriginal people affected.

1998 A referendum on a proposal to make Australia a republic is defeated.

2000 The 2000 Olympics prove a great success and are lauded as the best ever. As a result, Australia's global reputation is greatly enhanced.

2001 Australian government pledges almost unbridled support for the USA after the terrorist attack on 11 September and commits troops to the invasion of Iraq.

2002 The nation mourns as 88 of its citizens are killed in a nightclub bombing in Bali, Indonesia.

2005 Racially motivated violence, involving thousands of youths, hits Sydney. Despite widespread concern, it is passed off as an inevitable symptom – and minor aberration – of a developing cosmopolitan immigrant population.

2006 With the country in the grip of the worst drought on record, the government slashes economic growth forecasts, reflecting a slump in farm output. John Howard declares water security to be Australia's biggest challenge, but still dismisses the Kyoto Climate Change Protocol and joins the USA in its refusal to sign. Meanwhile, Melbourne hosts the 18th Commonwealth Games.

2007 With the Iraq debacle still playing out, climate change a major election issue, and despite a booming resource-driven economy, Prime Minister John Howard suffers an embarrassing election defeat. For Howard it is an incredulous end to 11 years at the helm. The Australian public look to fresh policy direction and a more youthful leadership in the form of Labor leader and Prime Minister Kevin Rudd.

2008 Before the opening of parliament, Kevin Rudd gives a formal parliamentary apology to Aboriginal Australians and says 'Sorry' to the 'Stolen Generations'.

2009 Australia suffers its worst ever bush-fire season and environmental disaster, with 'Black Saturday' in Victoria claiming 173 lives.

2010 Thanks largely to continuing demand for its natural resources, Australia survives the worst of the global economic crisis.

Australian coat of arms above New Parliament House, Canberra

Politics

Since federation in 1901, Australia has maintained a stable democratic political system and remains a Commonwealth Realm. The capital city and seat of federal government is in Canberra, located in the Australian Capital Territory.

Due to the relatively young age of Australian politics, its history is not complex, but its structure is. Symbolic executive power is vested in the British monarch, represented throughout Australia by the governor-general.

The bicameral parliament consists of the queen, the senate (the upper house) and the house of representatives (the lower house).

Elections for both chambers are held every three years and voting is compulsory. There are three major political parties: the Liberal Party, the Australian Labor Party, and the National Party.

Which party, or where's the party?

The image of Australians as notoriously laid-back and ardent lovers of their enviable and seemingly uncomplicated outdoor lifestyle, together with the fact of a complex political system, has given rise to the perception that the vast majority of the bronzed and contented populace could not care less about politics. Lucky then (for the politicians anyway), that voting in Australia is compulsory.

Although there is perhaps some truth in this perception, Australians are undoubtedly becoming increasingly interested in politics. There is considerable debate as to why this may be so, but several factors seem to have broken the indifference and threatened the abiding sense of comfort. The debacle in Iraq plays a part. More and more, Australians feel some accountability is due and that the threat of terrorism in Australia and worldwide is increasing, not decreasing, as some politicians would vehemently proclaim. In the middle of the worst drought on record and with bush fires worsening in severity and scale, climate change is also a big issue. It is, after all, beginning to hurt. Additionally, the real-estate and rental markets, especially in Sydney, have created a widening gap between young and old, rich and poor. Even before the global economic crisis of 2008–9, the new social monikers were 'credit crunch' and 'mortgage stress'. All equating to a concerted desire for change.

'SORRY'

'Love', 'sorry' and 'hate': words loaded with meaning, motivation, despair and suffering, often overused, not meant or held back.

In Australia, the word 'sorry' has a special significance, and in February 2008 its reach became historic. For 100 years until 1969, under various state acts of parliament and enacted by Australian government agencies and church missions, an estimated 100,000 Australian Aboriginal and Torres Strait Islander children, usually of mixed descent, were removed from their families to become wards of state. The ideology and justification behind this act, let alone its ramifications, will be fiercely debated for decades, but it accelerated rather than eased the breakdown of Aboriginal culture in Australia. To the Aborigine, the sense of family is as vital a link to a sustainable existence as the sense of spirit, or connection to the land, and it served them well for over 40,000 years.

In 1995, a federal enquiry into the 'Stolen Generations' branded the policies as genocide and called for an official apology and compensation for those affected. Under the conservative leadership of John Howard between 1996 and 2007, an apology never materialised, despite major public protests.

On 13 February 2008, within three months of Howard's election loss, Kevin Rudd, the new prime minister, made an appointment with the nation and before the opening of parliament gave the parliamentary apology so many had waited for, for so long. Many underestimate the power of the simple word 'sorry', yet without its utterance – with integrity and in sincerity – most agree you can never truly move on.

In 2007, that change came, predictably yet dramatically, with the ousting of the Howard government after 11 years in power. On the eve of the global economic crisis, Labor's relatively youthful leader and polished Prime Minister Kevin Rudd assumed responsibility. Sound management and policy decisions saw a successful first term in office, and with the party's handling of the economy in particular – in effect, surviving the crisis relatively unscathed – it seems that Rudd and Labor look assured to continue into a second term.

The unofficial 'Aboriginal Embassy' opposite the Old Parliament Building, Canberra

Culture

Australia is often accused – especially by its colonial bedrock, England – of having two types of desert. One is outback and under oceanic skies; the other is cultural and has showers of beer. Of course, although in decades past this affectionate if provocative label may have held some truth, the reality is that for a country pretty isolated, with only 22 million people and with such a young (white) history, the culture is not only thriving, but world class.

That said, it is very important to note that Australia is (or was), of course, also home to one of the most impressive, complex and long-established cultures on earth: the Aboriginal. Though much of that culture is now lost, or presented in a highly commercial fashion, it is nonetheless well worth investigating deeper while you are there. In many ways, our modern culture is shallow, fleeting and meaningless compared to theirs and its sustainability suspect.

Even a summary of Aboriginal culture is beyond the scope of this book. Suffice to say that their culture and very existence was tried and tested over many thousands of years, resulting in great complexity, although in some ways it is admirable in its utter simplicity. Above all, until white colonisation, it was sustainable. Unlike our modern culture of music, art and language, theirs was intrinsic to everyday life, communication and evolution. It was not so much focused on mere entertainment and personal or group creativity as on a vital element of community and long-term survival. In many ways it was their lifeblood.

Music

Australia has a quality classical music and operatic scene, with the Opera House the showcase venue for the country's top orchestras and performers.

Matchsticks by Sydney artist Brett Whiteley

When it comes to contemporary popular music, Australia has played its part over recent decades, with INXS, AC/DC and Midnight Oil all being household names. Then, of course, there is pop diva Kylie Minogue, who has certainly come a long way from playing 'Charlene' in the popular Australian soap *Neighbours*. And unforgettable, too, were Men at Work, who in 1981 brought us Australia's second and unofficial national anthem, 'Down Under'. However, in 2010 this song was determined to have infringed the copyright of the traditional song 'Kookaburra', and the band has been ordered to pay royalties to the copyright holder.

Didgeridoos abound in Sydney's many souvenir shops

Dance

The Sydney Dance Company was founded in 1969 and, through the solid directorship of resident choreographer Graeme Murphy since 1976, it has become Australia's premier contemporary dance company and one of the country's most prolific and celebrated arts organisations. To date, it has had over 20 highly successful international tours.

Formed in 2001, the Bangarra Dance Theatre, also based in Sydney, is world renowned for its impressive blend of traditional Aboriginal and Torres Strait Island history and culture with international contemporary dance.

Film

Although born in the US, Mel Gibson grew up in Australia and is recognised by most as an Australian. His roles in such classics as *Mad Max*, *Lethal Weapon* and *Braveheart* made him a household name. Paul Hogan (aka *Crocodile Dundee*) also caused something of a phenomenon in 1986. But their prominence has now been overshadowed in no uncertain terms by the two acting greats Nicole Kidman and Russell Crowe.

In 2008 Nicole Kidman starred in the blockbuster *Australia* directed by Baz Luhrmann. The film centres on an English aristocrat in the 1930s (played by Kidman) who comes to outback Australia to sell a large cattle property. After an epic journey across the country with a rough-hewn drover (played by Australian actor Hugh Jackman), they are caught in the bombing of Darwin during World War II. The film was generally considered to be a success and did a great deal to enhance the country's tourist appeal.

Festivals and events

With a climate highly conducive to outdoor activities and a population largely based in coastal cities, Australia enjoys a rich and varied schedule of festivals and events. Most take place in the summer months and a great deal involve Australians' two great loves – sports and the beach. Many are well-established, high-profile annual events, while others are more low-key and localised, often celebrating some of life's great pleasures like food, wine or music. However, there is always something happening.

Sport and the great venues

Sydney and Melbourne are the focus for the most popular high-profile sports events, and their venues are globally iconic. In Sydney, Stadium Australia (*www.anzstadium.com.au*) has seen many a great sporting event since its role in the 2000 Olympics, and the Sydney Cricket Ground (SCG) (*www.sydneycricketground.com.au*) has a rich history. In Melbourne, it is 'The G' (Melbourne Cricket Ground, MCG) (*www.mcg.org.au*) that frequently roars to life with cries of 'Aussie, Aussie, Aussie'.

Everyone knows Australians are mad about cricket, and every summer there is an intense schedule of domestic and international matches in both cities, with the traditional Boxing Day test at the MCG attracting around 90,000 spectators. Other summer annuals of international significance are the Australian Open Tennis in January (*www.australianopen.com*) and the Grand Prix in March (*www.grandprix.com.au*), both staged in Melbourne. In winter, Australian Rules Football (AFL) (*www.afl.com.au*), Rugby Union (*www.rugby.com.au*), Rugby League (*www.nrl.com.au*) and to a lesser extent football (*www.footballaustralia.com.au*) dominate.

Cultural and historic

With a relatively infant colonial (non-Aboriginal) history, Australia makes a big thing of memorial days, with Australia Day on 26 January a classic. On that day, the flags and face paint, as well as the picnics and the stubbies (beers), seem omnipresent, with Sydney always stealing the show with its vast flotilla of boats out on the harbour.

Another classic is the colourful Sydney Gay and Lesbian Mardi Gras, held every February (*www.mardigras.org.au*). Although many events are involved, the highlight is the parade, where the city's proud and extrovert gay community puts on a spectacular show.

Arts and music are always a staple in the annual events calendar, and whether they are the majors like the Sydney Festival in January (*www.sydneyfestival.org.au*) and Melbourne International Arts Festival in October (*www.melbournefestival.com.au*), or more localised like the Point Nepean Music Festival (April), they are always of high quality with an impressive international attendance.

Life's a beach

Many events and festivals are held on the east coast's abundant beaches. On Bondi Beach in Sydney, both Christmas and New Year usually prove messy affairs, while in September the Festival of the Winds (a kite festival) at the same location is far more sedate. Elsewhere, just about every major beach and surf life-saving club up and down the coast will host an event during the summer months.

The 'race that stops a nation'

Australians love their horse racing and the Melbourne Spring Carnival in November is the biggest meeting of the racing year (*www.springracingcarnival.com.au*). Four race days are held over a week at the Flemington Racecourse, with the Melbourne Cup the main highlight. Billed as the 'race that stops a nation' and marked with a public holiday in Victoria, it is generally regarded as the most prestigious 'two-mile' handicap in the world. The Spring Carnival is also recognised as the principal social event in the Melbourne calendar, and ladies' fashion is a major feature, particularly on Oaks Day, the third race day. Like Melbourne Cup Day, it traditionally attracts over 100,000 punters.

Children prepare for a parade at the Womadelaide Music Festival, Adelaide

Highlights

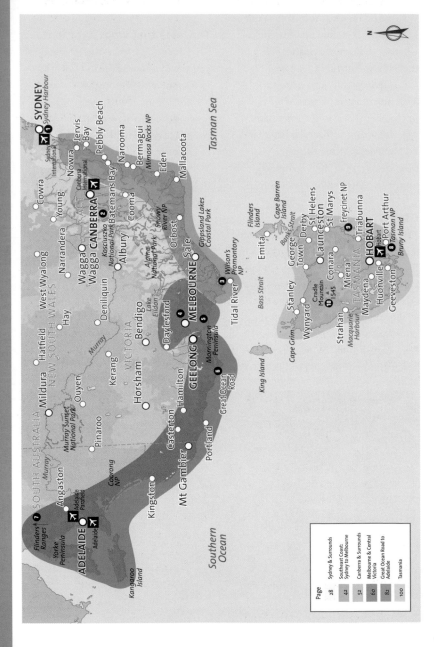

1 **Sydney Harbour** Stunning natural and man-made aesthetics combine to form one of the most beautiful natural harbours in the world. Your first encounter with the iconic Opera House and the Harbour Bridge is guaranteed to last a lifetime (*see p31*).

2 **Kosciuszko National Park** Home to Australia's highest mountain (the 2,228m/7,310ft Mount Kosciuszko) and arguably its best ski fields (*see pp58–9*).

3 **Wilson's Promontory National Park** The pride of Victoria's parks, 'The Prom' as it is known, possesses some of the most attractive and unspoilt coastal scenery anywhere along the east coast. A network of walking tracks, some taking several days to complete, makes it a haven for hikers (*see pp50–51*).

4 **Federation Square, Melbourne** Australia's answer to the Guggenheim Bilbao Museum or Pompidou Centre in Paris, the surreal and remarkable façade of 'Fed Square' is a powerful and effective draw for both Melbournians and tourists alike (*see p66*).

5 **Mornington Peninsula** Melbourne's very own coastal playground offers a fine mix of wild ocean beaches with the more sheltered ones of Port Phillip Bay. Home to the iconic colourful beach boxes, as well as some fine vineyards (*see pp72–3*).

6 **Great Ocean Road** The stretch of coastline between the Victorian towns of Torquay and Warrnambool is often billed as one of the most beautiful coastal drives in the world (*see pp82–3*).

7 **Flinders Ranges** South Australia's largest mountain range. The most characteristic landmark is Wilpena Pound, a huge natural amphitheatre covering nearly 80sq km (31sq miles) (*see pp98–9*).

8 **Tasman National Park and Port Arthur** Dramatic coastal scenery provides a suitable backdrop to the notorious former penal colony of Port Arthur (*see pp104–5*).

9 **Freycinet National Park** Arguably the most appealing coastal national park in Australia, with the idyllic swathe of white sand at Wineglass Bay its most alluring feature (*see p111*).

10 **Cradle Mountain** The most famous of Tasmania's many peaks and one of its most accessible. This is the gateway to the great Overland Track, Australia's most popular multi-day walk (*see p120 & pp122–3*).

Suggested itineraries

Given the size of Australia, combined with the fact you have already spent considerable time and money just getting here, time is of the essence. However, do not make the grave mistake of trying to do too much with the time you have, or your trip will inevitably turn into an exercise in frustration. Australia as a whole – and the southeast in particular – simply has too much to offer. It takes Australians months, sometimes years, to discover their own country, so don't for a minute think you can comprehensively do the job in a matter of days or weeks. The following offers a sample of some must-do sightseeing.

Sydney: long weekend

Day 1 Start with the sunrise at Macquarie Point, and then explore the Royal Botanic Gardens, the Opera House, Circular Quay, The Rocks and Harbour Bridge. After all that activity, rest your feet over a beer in the Lord Nelson pub followed by dinner down at the quayside.

Day 2 First a visit to the zoo, then a dip at Balmoral Beach, or visit the eclectic sights of Darling Harbour, with some retail therapy along George Street. For the more energetic, try the famed 'Bridge Climb'. In the evening, try your luck at the casino or take in a performance at the Opera House.

Day 3 Head to Bondi Beach, taking in the clifftop walk to Bronte, or escape the crowds with a harbour walk from Cremorne to Bradley's Head. Not into walking? Then take the ferry to Manly. That evening, head to Doyle's Restaurant in Watson's Bay, or see the sunset over the city from North Head.

Melbourne: long weekend

Day 1 Start your first day in Melbourne on a high, literally, with the great city views from the observation deck of the Eureka Tower. Better still, organise a balloon flight across the city at dawn. Back down to earth, enjoy a stroll through the Royal Botanic Gardens via Federation Square. Spend the rest of the day on the beach at St Kilda.

Day 2 Begin with a trip to Carlton Gardens and the Melbourne Museum, followed by some serious shopping in Melbourne Central, the Queen Victoria Market and the Bourke Street Mall. Alternatively, escape the city centre and visit the formal gardens and villages of the Dandenong Ranges National Park. Later, dine in one of the city's restaurants in Carlton or Fitzroy or at Mount Dandenong's Sky High restaurant.

Day 3 Catch a ferry from Southgate to Williamstown. Enjoy lunch in one of its many street-side cafés before catching the ferry back to Docklands. In the evening, take in a performance at the Regent Theatre, or try your luck at the Crown Casino.

A bird's-eye view of Melbourne from the Eureka Tower

The crystal-clear waters of Little Oberon Bay, Wilson's Promontory National Park

One to two weeks

With only one or two weeks in Australia, try to get the best of both urban and rural attractions. Give yourself at least a long weekend exploring one or two of the state capitals: Sydney, Melbourne, Adelaide or even Canberra. Then focus on short trips, perhaps five days, taking in the lower half of Tasmania (including Hobart and Port Arthur), Mornington Peninsula or the Great Ocean Road. Be sure to visit some of the best national parks like the Blue Mountains, Wilson's Promontory or, in winter, Kosciuszko.

Three to four weeks

Three to four weeks will certainly allow you to take in at least two of the main capitals. Compare the largest, Sydney and Melbourne, with Canberra or Adelaide. A road trip from Sydney to Melbourne, taking in the New South Wales south coast and Canberra, is recommended or, alternatively, from Melbourne on the Great Ocean Road to Adelaide. You will need at least ten days to see the major sights in Tasmania – and that's if the weather is kind. National parks and day trips like Daylesford from Melbourne, or the Barossa Valley from Adelaide, are also recommended.

Longer visits

Visits of more than a month allow you to become fully acquainted with Sydney and Melbourne, with a week in both and shorter stays in Adelaide and Canberra. Around Sydney, include one to three days in the Blue Mountains, and from Melbourne go on extended trips to the Mornington Peninsula, Dandenong Ranges, Wilson's Promontory and Phillip Island. Tasmania can be given at least two weeks, preferably three, if you include a multi-day walk. A week exploring the Great Ocean Road to Adelaide is recommended, and then from Adelaide try a taste of true outback with a trip to the Flinders Ranges.

Watching the sun set over the Twelve Apostles

Sydney

In the modern age of media hype and global marketing excess, Australia's largest and most celebrated city is one of a decreasing number of iconic destinations that actually lives up to its glowing reputation. You would be hard pressed to find anybody who has made its acquaintance and not left a loyal friend. While Paris and London have their culture and history, and New York its sheer scale, the key to Sydney's winning formula is without doubt its natural beauty and climate.

With much of the city built around a vast, complex natural harbour and its entire eastern flank one long urban oceanfront, the setting could hardly be more beautiful. Add to that a near-perfect climate and the instantly recognisable icons of the Opera House and Harbour Bridge, and there could be nothing more effective in putting Australia on the world map.

With a diverse population of 4 million, the pulse of Sydney is a strong one. It is brash, colourful and happening, even a tad arrogant. Sydney is the country's greatest urban draw and the principal gateway to the East Coast, and as such, tourism plays a fundamentally important role in the city's economy.

For the tourist Sydney offers a veritable wealth of things to see and do, many of which are fully deserving of that overused 'world-class' label. It boasts all the usual suspects – top-quality restaurants, retail outlets, historical and cultural sights and

attractions – but it also offers more unusual possibilities, like the Harbour Bridge Climb (*see p32*), stunning harbour walks (*see p31*), and its fair share of great annual festivals like the colourful Gay and Lesbian Mardi Gras.

For more information and bookings contact the **Sydney Visitor Centre** (*Level 1, corner of Argyle St & Playfair St, The Rocks. Tel: 1800 067 676 & (02) 9240 8788. www.visitnsw.com. Open: 9.30am–5.30pm*).

If there is one criticism to be levelled at Sydney, it is its size and all the social and logistical problems that come with it. While it is hardly as manic as Tokyo or Shanghai, this is not a city for the faint-hearted, as getting from A to B can be an ordeal. That said, the public transport system, which combines bus, train and ferry services, is well set up for visitors, with various discounted and combination fare structures. For information about all public transport, contact the **Transport Infoline** (*Tel: 131500. www.131500.info*).

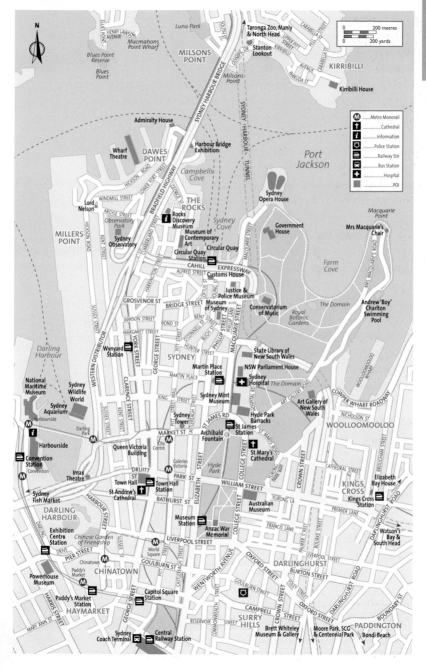

Beat that and there really is only one overriding problem left for the average overseas visitor: the paucity of time you inevitably have to experience the place. Planning is therefore important. Don't make the common mistake of extending your stay in Sydney to the detriment of the rest of the southeast. Bear in mind that this is just the area's urban offerings. Out there is an even more impressive natural world awaiting your acquaintance. This is just the start.

Circular Quay and The Rocks
Museum of Contemporary Art

Located between Circular Quay and The Rocks, the grand Art Deco Museum of Contemporary Art houses a collection of some of Australia's best modern works, together with works by renowned international artists such as Warhol and Hockney. The museum also hosts regular national and international exhibitions.

The in-house café overlooking the quay is also popular.

140 George St, The Rocks.
Tel: (02) 9245 2400. www.mca.com.au.
Open: daily 10am–5pm. Tours: Mon–Fri
11am & 1pm, Sat & Sun noon &
1.30pm. Free admission. Ferry, bus &
train: Circular Quay.

The Rocks

The Rocks village was the first site settled by European convicts and troops as early as 1788 and is the oldest part of the city. It was once the haunt of prostitutes, drunks and criminals, but although its social fabric has certainly changed, it still retains much of its original architectural charm. The area now serves as one of Sydney's most popular attractions, with an eclectic array of shops, galleries, arcades, cafés, old pubs and restaurants. See *www.therocks.com*

The popular **Rocks Market** (*George St & Playfair St, The Rocks. Open: Sat &*

Sydney Harbour Bridge, with the Opera House in the distance

Sun 10am–5pm) features contemporary arts, crafts and souvenirs. The 90-minute **Rocks Walking Tour** is an excellent way to learn about the torrid history of the area (*Tours depart from 23 Playfair St, The Rocks. Tel: (02) 9247 6678. www.rockswalkingtours.com.au*).

Nearby in Kendal Lane, the **Rocks Discovery Museum** (*Tel: (02) 9240 8680. www.rocksdiscoverymuseum.com.au. Open: 10am–5pm. Free admission*) houses interactive historical exhibits.

To escape the crowds and see some fine views, head up Argyle St to **Observatory Park**, which is also home to the **Sydney Observatory** (*Tel: (02) 9921 3485. www.sydneyobservatory.com.au. Admission charge*), Australia's oldest, where tours are available.

Sydney Harbour Bridge

Affectionately nicknamed 'The Coathanger', the Sydney Harbour Bridge is one of the greatest urban constructions in the world. Opened in 1932, having taken nine years to build and reaching 134m (440ft) in height, it supports eight lanes of traffic (accommodating up to 175,000 vehicles a day), a railway line and a pedestrian walkway. Until recently, the best views from the bridge were accessed by foot from its 59m-high (194ft) deck, but now the 'Bridge Climb' experience has become a world-famous Sydney 'must-do' (*see p32*).

There are also (far cheaper) views on offer from the top of the southeastern

Pylon Lookout, accessed from the eastern walkway and Cumberland St, The Rocks. The pylon also houses the **Harbour Bridge Exhibition** (*Open: 10am–5pm. Tel: (02) 9240 1100. www.pylonlookout.com. Admission charge*). From below, the best views of the bridge can be enjoyed from Hickson Rd and Dawes Point Park (south side) and Milsons Point (north side).

Sydney Opera House

Completed in 1973 and now arguably Australia's most recognised (man-made) icon, the Sydney Opera House cannot fail to impress. Its intriguing, shell-like façades house five performance venues ranging from the main 2,690-capacity Concert Hall to the small Playhouse Theatre. Combined, they host about 2,500 performances annually. The Opera House is the principal performance venue for Opera Australia, the Australian Ballet, the Sydney Symphony Orchestra and the Sydney Theatre Company. Bookings for tours, performances and packages are essential and available online. Cafés, bars, a restaurant and a store are also located within the complex. On summer evenings the bars below the main complex must surely be one of the best places on the planet for a convivial beer or G&T.
Via Macquarie St, Circular Quay. Tel: (02) 9250 7777. www.soh.nsw.gov.au. Open: daily 9am–8.30pm. Free admission, tours extra. Ferry, bus & train: Circular Quay.

Sydney activities

Harbour Bridge Climb
Without doubt the highest-profile activity in Sydney is the award-winning Bridge Climb, a 3-hour ascent of the 134m (440ft) Harbour Bridge. It can be undertaken day or night and the harbour views are spectacular. Note, however, that for safety reasons you cannot take your own camera on the trip.
5 Cumberland St, The Rocks.
Tel: (02) 8274 7777.
www.bridgeclimb.com.
Open: 7am–7pm. Admission charge.

Harbour cruises
There is a vast array on offer, with most based at Circular Quay and Darling Harbour. Trips vary from dinner cruises on paddle steamers to scenic trips on fast catamarans and even jet-boat rides. The Sydney Visitor Centre (*see p28*) and Harbourside Information Desk (*Level 2, Harbourside Shopping Centre. Tel: (02) 9281 3999. www.darlingharbour.com.au*) have details and take bookings. Note that a multiple-trip ferry ticket is a perfectly good and far cheaper alternative.

Sailing
Sydney Harbour offers some of the best sailing in the world.

Sydney Mainsail (*Tel: (02) 9719 9077. www.sydneymainsail.com.au*) offers 3-hour trips with highly experienced skippers. **Australian Spirit Sailing Company** (*Tel: (02) 9878 0300. www.austspiritsailingco. com.au*) and **Sydney by Sail** based at the National Maritime Museum (*Tel: (02) 9280 1110. www.sydneybysail. com*) are two other alternatives; the latter runs social day trips and introductory lessons.

'Bridge climbers' trek up the steep incline of the Sydney Harbour Bridge

Scenic flights

Both fixed-wing and helicopter scenic flights are available.
Sydney Heli-Aust (*Bankstown Airport. Tel: (02) 9791 0322. www.heliaust.com.au*) offers pickups from the city. **Palm Beach Seaplanes** (*Rose Bay & Palm Beach. Tel: 1300 720 995. www.sydneybyseaplane.com.au*) offers an interesting alternative. Flight times range from 15 to 60 minutes.

There are also some options for the more adventurous, including **Red Baron Scenic Flights** (*Tel: (02) 9791 0643. www.redbaron.com.au*), offering an unforgettable aerobatic scenic harbour flight in an open cockpit. Then there is the antithesis: ballooning. **Cloud 9** (*Tel: 1300 555 711. www.cloud9balloonflights.com*) and **Balloon Aloft** (*Tel: 1800 028 568. www.balloonaloft.com*) both offer early morning flights over the outer suburbs or in the Hunter Valley.

Sea kayaking

The vast harbour lends itself to kayaking and you can literally lose yourself for hours in the many bays and tributaries. Kayaks can be hired from **Sydney Harbour Kayaks** (*3/235 Spit Rd, Mosman. Tel: (02) 9960 4389. www.sydneyharbourkayaks.com.au*).

Surfing

Manly and Bondi are the places to hire boards and have lessons. Try the **Manly Surf School** for good-value, 11am–1pm daily classes (*North Steyne Surf Club, Manly Beach. Tel: (02) 9977 6977. www.manlysurfschool.com*). In Bondi try **Let's Go Surfing** (*128 Ramsgate Ave North, Bondi. Tel: (02) 9365 1800*).

Swimming

The ocean beaches at Bondi, Bronte, Clovelly and Coogee are recommended, while to the north, Manly, Collaroy, Narrabeen, Avalon, Ocean Beach and Palm Beach are also good spots. Lifeguards patrol most beaches in summer, but make sure you always swim between the yellow and red flags.

SYDNEY TRAVEL PASSES

The **Day-Tripper Pass** gives all-day access to trains, buses and ferries, and can be purchased at any rail, bus or ferry sales or information outlet or on buses. The **Travel Pass** allows unlimited, weekly or quarterly combined travel throughout designated zones or sections. For the tourist, **The Sydney Pass** is a good bet, offering unlimited travel on ferries and standard buses as well as on the Sydney and Bondi Explorer routes and the four STA Harbour Cruises. They are sold as three-day, five-day or seven-day passes. Discount, ten-trip 'Travel Ten' (bus) and 'Ferry Ten' (ferry) passes are also recommended.
Tel: 131 500. www.131500.info

City centre
Hyde Park and surrounds

Located alongside the Central Business District and graced with spacious lawns and mighty corridors of trees, Hyde Park is a magnet for city suits at lunchtime. The 1932 **Archibald Fountain** and 1934 **Anzac War Memorial** are its main historical features. Nearby stands the impressive **St Mary's Cathedral**. Free tours run on Sunday afternoons after midday Mass (*College St. Tel: (02) 9220 0400. Free admission. Explorer bus: stop 5*).

The **Australian Museum**, established in 1827, is well up with the play of technology, presentation and entertainment, with the biodiversity and indigenous Australian displays being of particular note. Children are also well catered for in the state-of-the-art 'Search and Discover' section and 'Kidspace', a mini museum for the under-fives (*6 College St. Tel: (02) 9320 6000. www.australianmuseum.net.au. Open: 9.30am–5pm. Admission charge, and special exhibitions extra. Explorer bus: stop 6*).

Macquarie Street

Along with The Rocks, Macquarie is the historical hub of the city and retains many of its most significant and impressive colonial buildings.

From north to south, the first, surrounded by its own expansive grounds, is the 1837 **Government House**. The interior contains many period furnishings and features giving

The Museum of Sydney, dwarfed by modern high-rises

an insight into the lifestyle of the former NSW governors and their families (*Tel: (02) 9931 5222. Open: Fri–Sun 10.30am–3pm, grounds 10am–4pm. Free admission & guided tours*).

Further along is the **State Library of New South Wales**, housing some very significant historical documents, including eight out of the ten known First Fleet diaries, as well as visiting exhibitions. There's a shop and café on site (*Tel: (02) 9273 1414. www.sl.nsw.gov.au. Open: Mon–Thur 9am–8pm, Fri 9am–5pm, Sat & Sun 10am–5pm. Admission charge for visiting exhibitions*).

Next door to the library is the **NSW Parliament House**. Free tours are available when parliament is not in session (*www.parliament.nsw.gov.au*).

The former 1816 **Hyde Park Barracks** lie on the northern fringe of

Hyde Park and now house a modern museum displaying their history and the work of the architect Francis Greenway. Tours are available and there's a café on site.
Macquarie St. Tel: (02) 8239 2311. www.hht.nsw.gov.au. Open: 9.30am–5pm. Admission charge. Explorer bus: stop 4.

Museum of Sydney

Built on the original site of Governor Phillip's (the captain of the 'First Fleet') former 1788 residence, the MOS explores the history and stories that surround the creation and development of the city. Shop and café on site.
37 Phillip St. Tel: (02) 9251 5988. www.hht.nsw.gov.au. Open: 9.30am– 5pm. Admission charge.

Queen Victoria Building (QVB)

Taking up an entire city block, the grand Queen Victoria Building was built in 1898 to celebrate Queen Victoria's Golden Jubilee. Amid the ornate architecture, stained-glass windows, mosaics and two charming

and intricate Automata Turret Clocks are three floors of modern boutiques, galleries, restaurants and cafés.
455 George St. Tel: (02) 9267 4761. www.qvb.com.au. Open: daily, guided tours twice daily (Tel: (02) 9264 9209). Explorer bus: stop 14.

Sydney (Centrepoint) Tower

Rising from the heart of the Central Business District, the 250m (820ft) Sydney Tower has, since 1981, been an instantly recognisable landmark across the city. As well as the expansive vistas from the tower's **Observation Deck** (*Open: daily 9am–10.30pm. Admission charge*), you can also experience **OzTrek**, a virtual reality ride across Australia (*Extra admission charge*), or dine in one of two revolving restaurants. The more adventurous can even venture outdoors and experience **Skywalk**, a glass-floored platform (*Open: 9.30am–8.45pm. Tel: (02) 9333 9200. www.skywalk.com.au. Admission charge*).
100 Market St. Tel: (02) 9333 9222. Explorer bus: stop 14.

Sydney skyline viewed from the Opera House

East of the centre
Art Gallery of New South Wales

At the southeastern corner of the Royal Botanic Gardens is this, Australia's largest gallery. Housed behind its grand façade are permanent works of contemporary Australian artists, an impressive international collection and the Yiribana Gallery, dedicated to works by Aboriginals and Torres Strait Islanders. Half-hour dance and music performances add to the experience.
Art Gallery Rd, Domain.
Tel: (02) 9225 1744.
www.artgallery.nsw.gov.au. Open: 10am–5pm. Free admission. Explorer bus: stop 12.

Bondi Beach

The most famous of Sydney's many ocean beaches and the epitome of the great Sydney lifestyle. Behind the beach, Bondi's bustling waterfront offers a tourist trap of cafés, restaurants, bars, surf and souvenir shops. To the south, **Bronte Beach** connects with Bondi Beach via a popular scenic clifftop walkway.
Bus: 321, 322, 365, 366, 380 from Circular Quay. Rail: from Circular Quay to Bondi Junction (Illawara Line), then bus (numbers above).

Eastern suburbs

Situated near the Navy's Woolloomooloo docks, **Kings Cross** (or 'the Cross' as it is nicknamed) has been the hub of the city's nightlife for decades. For some it is totally overrated, but others end up staying there for weeks. There is really only one way to find out if it's your scene.

Located close to the Cross is **Elizabeth Bay House**, a revival-style estate built in 1845 (*7 Onslow Ave, Elizabeth Bay. Tel: (02) 9356 3022. Open: Tue–Sun 10am–4.30pm. Admission charge. Explorer bus: stop 9*). The interior is restored and faithfully furnished in accordance with the times, and the house has a great outlook across the harbour.

Just south of the Cross, **Darlinghurst** and **Surry Hills** offer a wealth of fine restaurants and cafés. In Surry Hills don't miss the **Brett Whiteley Museum and Gallery**, the former studio and home of one of Sydney's most popular contemporary artists, who died in 1992 (*2 Raper St. Tel: 1800 679 278. Open: 10am–4pm. Admission charge*).

Sydney's famous Bondi Beach

Sydney's Royal Botanic Gardens contrast with the city office blocks

The big attraction in **Paddington** is **Oxford St**, one of the most happening areas of the city, and a conglomerate of cheap eateries, cafés, restaurants, clubs and bars. It is also a major focus for the city's gay community. The colourful **Paddington Market** is held every Saturday from 10am (*395 Oxford St. Tel: (02) 9331 2923*). Just to the south of Paddington, Moore Park is home to the famous **Sydney Cricket Ground** (*Tours tel: (02) 9380 0383. Explorer bus: stop 16*). Further south again is **Centennial Park**, which at 220ha (544 acres) is Sydney's largest.

Watson's Bay, sitting on the leeward side of South Head, which guards the mouth of Sydney Harbour, offers some fine short walks and historic points of interest and is home to the famous **Doyles Seafood Restaurant** (*Tel: (02) 9337 2007. Ferry: from Circular Quay Wharfs 2 & 4. Bus: 325 & 342 from Circular Quay*).

Royal Botanic Gardens
A short stroll from the city centre, the 30ha (74-acre), 200-year-old Royal Botanic Gardens boast a fine array of mainly native plants and trees, rose and succulent gardens, a Tropical House (*Admission charge*), decorative ponds and a resident colony of flying foxes (bats). There is also a visitor centre, shop, café and restaurant (*Tel: (02) 9231 8050*). From the Botanic Gardens it is a short stroll via Mrs Macquarie's Rd to **Macquarie Point**, which offers one of the best vistas of the Opera House and Harbour Bridge (*Explorer bus: stop 5*). *Art Gallery Rd. Tel: (02) 9231 8111. www.rbgsyd.nsw.gov.au. Open: 7am–sunset; guided walks daily 10.30am & 1pm. Free admission. Explorer bus: stop 4.*

The North Shore and city outskirts

Manly

Manly is more resort than suburb and offers a great day away from the city centre. Its famous surf beach is very much the main attraction, together with a happening restaurant and café scene. The one letdown is its rather tacky 'Corso' pedestrian precinct, but this is now being outclassed by the fast-developing wharf and waterfront areas. Other main tourist attractions are the **Oceanworld** aquarium complex (*Tel: (02) 8251 7877. www.oceanworld.com.au. Open: 10am–5.30pm. Admission charge*) and the **Manly Art Gallery and Museum** (*Tel: (02) 9976 1420. Open: Tue–Sun 10am–5pm. Free admission*), both located just west of the wharf.

A visit to the tip of the **North Head** peninsula (just south of Manly) is very worthwhile, particularly at sunset. The views across the harbour towards the city are spectacular. Just follow Scenic Drive to the very end. The **Quarantine Station** (*Tel: (02) 9466 1551. www.q-station.com.au. Admission charge for tours*), which takes up a large portion of the peninsula, was used from 1832 to harbour ships known to be carrying diseases such as smallpox or bubonic plague. The station closed in 1984 and is now administered as a historical site by the NSW Parks and Wildlife Service. Two-hour tours are available, as are

Palm Beach, one of many beaches on Sydney's beautiful North Shore

three-hour 'Ghost Tours' and two-hour 'Family Tours'. Call or check the website for the latest schedules.

Northern beaches
The coast north of Manly is inundated with picturesque bays and fine surf beaches that stretch 40km (25 miles) to Barrenjoey Head and the mighty Hawkesbury River harbour. Not surprisingly, this area is the location of some extremely sought-after suburban real estate. Perhaps the most popular of the beaches are Narrabeen, Avalon and Whale Beach, but there are many to choose from.

At the very tip is **Barrenjoey Head**, crowned by a historic lighthouse built in 1881. Nearby is the beautiful **Palm Beach**, made famous as the principal filming location for the Aussie soap *Home and Away*. Day cruises up the **Hawkesbury River** or shorter excursions to the **Ku-ring-gai Chase National Park** are available from the **Palm Beach Public Wharf** (*Tel: (02) 9974 2411. Bus: 90 from Wynard to Palm Beach*).

Taronga Zoo
Set harbourside and amid the most expensive real estate in Australia, Taronga can certainly boast one of the best locations and views of any zoo in the world. Going back as far as 1881, the institution is an old one and as such has built up an extensive species list that includes the obligatory koala, platypus, marsupials and colourful Australian birds. The more traditional

Sydney's Taronga Zoo

residents are also in evidence and include gorilla, tiger, bear, giraffe, the largest captive troop of chimps in the world, and a large new elephant enclosure. You will almost certainly need a full day to explore the various exhibits on offer and there are plenty of events staged throughout the day to keep both adults and children entertained. The best of these is without doubt the Free Flight Bird Show, staged twice daily in an open-air arena overlooking the city.

A Zoo Pass combo ticket includes ferry transfers and zoo entry.
Tel: (02) 9969 2777. www.zoo.nsw.gov.au. Open: 9am–5pm. Admission charge. Ferry: from Circular Quay Wharf 2, quarter past and quarter to the hour 7.15am–6.45pm.

Tour: Blue Mountains

Less than two hours' drive west of Sydney, the 'Blueys' (as they are affectionately known) contain five national parks covering a total area of 10,000sq km (3,860sq miles). A network of eroded river valleys, gorges and bluffs offer a vast wonderland of natural features, from precipitous cliffs to dramatic waterfalls. The 'blue' label derives from the visual effects of sunlight on oils released by the vast swathes of eucalyptus forest.

Allow a whole day for the 279km (173-mile) route.

From the centre of Sydney, take the M4 (toll) west to Glenbrook.

1 Glenbrook

Located just beyond the Nepean River, the small village of Glenbrook is considered the gateway to the Blue Mountains. From the northern end of the village follow signs to **Lennox Bridge**, the oldest in Australia, built by convicts in 1833. Nearby **Knapsack Park** offers fine views back towards Sydney, though this is just a taste of better things to come.
From Glenbrook, continue west on the Western Highway (SH32) to Wentworth Falls.

2 Wentworth Falls

The stunning lookouts across **Wentworth Falls** and the **Jamieson Valley** (signposted off SH32) offer a dramatic introduction to the classic scenery of the Blue Mountains. Walking tracks take in viewpoints around the falls, and the **Den Fenella Track** will

take you to some good lookouts.
From Wentworth Falls, continue west on the Western Highway (SH32) to Katoomba.

3 Katoomba and around

Considered the capital of the Blue Mountains, the historic town of Katoomba is an interesting mix of old and new, with its tourism highlight being the **Three Sisters** lookout at **Echo Point**, the Blueys' most famous. From the lookout it is possible to walk around to the stacks and descend the taxing **Giant Stairway Walk** to the valley floor (30 minutes). The **Katoomba Visitor Information Centre** is at Echo Point (*Tel: 1300 653 408. www.visitbluemountains.com.au. Open: 9am–5pm*).

West of Echo Point is the highly commercial **Scenic World**, with various unusual scenic transportation opportunities (*junction of Cliff Drive and Violet St. Tel: 1300 759 9255.*

www.scenicworld.com.au. Open:
9am–5pm. Admission charge).
From Katoomba, continue northwest on
the Western Highway (SH32) to
Blackheath.

4 Blackheath

The sleepy little village of Blackheath is especially popular in autumn when the tree-lined streets turn to gold. But year-round it is **Evans** and **Govetts Leap** lookouts that provide the aesthetic drama. An added attraction is **Bridal Veil Falls**, the highest in the Blue Mountains. The lookouts are all signposted from the village.

Continue on SH32 to Mount Victoria
then turn right following signs to Bell.
At Bell turn left (west) on SH40
to Clarence.

5 Zig Zag Railway and the Bells Line of Road

Clarence forms the terminus of the Zig Zag Railway. Originally built in 1866, restored steam trains now make the 8km (5-mile), 1½-hour journey to Bottom Points (*Tel: (02) 6355 2955.*
www.zigzagrailway.com.au. Trains: daily
(steam trains on Sat, Sun & Wed) 11am,
1pm & 3pm. Journey fare).
Returning east on SH40 (the Bells Line
of Road), follow the northern rim of the
Grose Valley. This will take you back to
Sydney via Richmond and Windsor.
The main point of interest is the 28ha
(69-acre) cool-climate **Sydney (Mount**
Tomah) Botanic Garden, *home to over*
10,000 species (Tel: (02) 4567 2154.
www.rbgsyd.nsw.gov.au. Open:
10am–4pm. Admission charge).

Tour: Blue Mountains

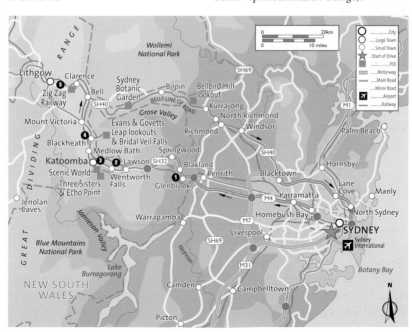

Southeast coast: Sydney to Melbourne

With all the tourist hype surrounding Byron Bay, the Gold Coast and Cairns, the vast majority of international visitors dutifully head north from Sydney leaving the southeast of New South Wales and the east coast of Victoria primarily the domain of domestic holidaymakers, mainly Canberrians. Few, therefore, are aware of just how beautiful this area is.

In this small corner of New South Wales there are over 35 national parks and nature reserves, which is more than any other region in the state; the coastal aesthetics are easily on a par with anything between Sydney and the Queensland border. The pace of life here is also far less frenetic. Indeed, it is so laid-back that even the roos hang out at the beach!

South of Sydney, the New South Wales coast is split into four quite distinct regions: Wollongong and Kiama; the Shoalhaven Coast, which extends from Nowra to Bateman's Bay; the Eurobodalla Coast, which stretches from Bateman's Bay to Narooma; and the Sapphire Coast, which idles its way to the Victorian border. From there, the A1 skirts the remote Croajingolong National Park and coastal lakes of east Gippsland before delivering you at Wilson's Promontory, the southernmost tip of mainland Australia and one of the most celebrated and appealing coastal national parks in the country. Provided you can drag yourself away from The Prom's pristine beaches, it is then only a few hours' scenic drive to Melbourne.

SYDNEY TO BATEMAN'S BAY
Wollongong

Wollongong is the third-largest city in New South Wales, and without doubt its greatest assets are its beaches. Either side of Flagstaff Point there are almost 20 stretching from the Royal National Park in the north to Bass Point in the south, all providing excellent opportunities for sunbathing, swimming and surfing. In the city, the **Wollongong City Gallery** is one of the best regional galleries in the state (*Corner of Kembla and Burelli Sts. Tel: (02) 4228 7500. www.wollongongcitygallery.com. Open: Tue–Fri 10am–5pm, Sat & Sun noon–4pm. Free admission*).

Nan Tien Buddhist Temple

This temple, south of the city centre, is the largest in the Southern Hemisphere. It is open to visitors and offers tours,

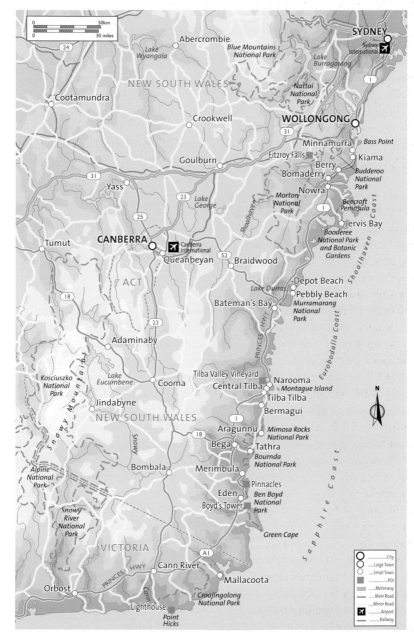

accommodation and a varied programme of weekend workshops (*Berkeley Rd, Berkeley. Tel: (02) 4272 0600. www.nantien.org.au. Open: Tue–Sun 9am–5pm. Admission charge*). *The Wollongong Visitor Information Centre. 93 Crown St. Tel: (02) 4227 5545. www.tourismwollongong.com.au. Open: Mon–Fri 9am–5pm, Sat 9am–4pm, Sun 10am–4pm.*

Kiama, Minnamurra and Berry

Kiama heralds what is the first of many pretty coastal townships dotted along the coast to the Victorian border. Most activity centres on Blowhole Point, crowned by its 1887 lighthouse. The blowhole is particularly active during a southeasterly.

Inland, 10km (6 miles) west of Kiama, is the **Minnamurra Rainforest**, which forms part of the **Budderoo National Park**. The National Parks and Wildlife Service visitor centre serves as the base for several walking tracks exploring the forest and Minnamurra Falls (*Off Jamberoo Mountain Rd. Tel: (02) 4236 0469. www.nationalparks.nsw.gov.au. Open: 9am–5pm. Vehicle entry admission charge. Café and shop*).

Roughly halfway between Kiama and Nowra is the delightful village of Berry with its attractive craft shops and cafés. The façade of the **Great Southern Hotel Motel** (*95 Queen St, Berry. Tel: (02) 4464 1009*) also stands out, but its quirkiness is not confined to the exterior. The centrepiece inside the bar is a World War I torpedo set proudly above the pool table. During the great Pacific nuclear testing hiatus in the mid-1990s, the torpedo was apparently rammed at admirable speed into the gates of the French Embassy in Canberra atop a Volkswagen Beetle. Only in Australia!

Jervis Bay and the Booderee National Park

Beyond Berry you reach the Shoalhaven River, twin towns of Nowra and Bomaderry and the start of the Shoalhaven Coast region. Before hitting the coast proper you may like to investigate the **Fleet Air Arm Museum** just south of Nowra. With a 6,000sq m (64,500sq ft) exhibition centre it is the country's largest aviation museum (*Tel: (02) 4424 1920. www. shoalhavenmuseums.com.au/faam.htm. Open: 10am–4pm. Admission charge*).

The true magic of the region is revealed in and around Jervis Bay, which sits neatly between the Beecroft Peninsula to the north and the exquisite Booderee National Park to the south. The bay is particularly noted for its beautiful white beaches, dolphin-watching and world-class dive sites, while the national park offers a wealth of fine secluded beaches, campsites, bush walks, stunning coastal scenery and a rich array of wildlife. Also located within the park are the **Booderee Botanic Gardens**, established in 1951 and an adjunct of the National Botanic Gardens in Canberra.

View from the Mount Keira lookout south towards Wollongong

*For local information, visit the
Shoalhaven Visitor Information Centre.
Corner of Princes Hwy and Pleasant
Way, Nowra. Tel: (02) 4421 0778.
www.shoalhaven.nsw.gov.au.
Open: 9am–5pm.
For national park information, access
and camping permits, contact the
visitor centre at the park entrance.
Village Rd. Tel: (02) 4443 0977.
www.booderee.np.gov.au. Open:
9am–4pm. Admission charge.*

Murramarang National Park

Located just north of Bateman's Bay,
Murramarang National Park is best
known for its tame and extremely
laid-back population of Eastern Grey
kangaroos, which frequent the
campsites and beaches. On occasion,
they are even known to cool off in the
surf. Other than the resident
marsupials, the coastal scenery here is
superb, with Pebbly Beach and Depot
Beach in the southern sector of the
park the most popular spots. Both have
campsites. A network of coast and

forest walks is also available, including
the popular 'Discovery Trail' off North
Durras Road, which skirts the edge of
Durras Lake.
*Access to Pebbly Beach is via the unsealed
Mount Agony Rd off the Princes Hwy
10km (6 miles) north of Bateman's Bay.
Depot Beach and Durras North are
accessed via North Durras Rd off Mount
Agony Rd. Admission charge for day-use
vehicle entry.*

BATEMAN'S BAY TO THE VICTORIAN BORDER
Bateman's Bay

The bustling and fast-developing
township of Bateman's Bay is 298km
(185 miles) south of Sydney, 146km
(91 miles) east of Canberra and 247km
(153 miles) north of the Victorian
border. It acts as the unofficial capital
of the New South Wales south coast
and is a popular spot for holidaymakers
from Canberra. For those on the way to
Melbourne, it is an ideal overnight stop
or base from which to explore the
immediate area, including the bay's best

beaches located southeast of the town centre. The area also has some excellent sea kayaking, horse trekking and diving. The visitor information centre can assist with bookings (*Corner of Princes Hwy and Beach Rd. Tel: (02) 4472 6900. www.eurobodalla.com.au. Open: 9am–5pm*).

Narooma and the Tilbas

Set on a headland beside the Wagonga River inlet, Narooma is 50km (31 miles) south of Bateman's Bay and has easy access to some lovely rocky beaches, national parks and the area's biggest attraction, **Montague Island**. A designated nature reserve about 8km (5 miles) offshore, the island is rich in wildlife with fur seals and seabirds making the island their home. Between October and December, humpback whales can be seen on their annual migration. The island has an interesting Aboriginal and European history and is crowned by a lighthouse built in 1881. The National Parks and Wildlife Service and several independent charters offer half-day tours and accommodation packages. Book at the visitor information centre (*Northern end of town, off the Princes Hwy. Tel: (02) 4476 2881. www.eurobodalla.com.au. Open: 9am–5pm*).

South of Narooma, in the shadow of Mount Dromedary, are the historic villages of Central Tilba and Tilba Tilba. Worth a visit, they have some of the south coast's best cafés and arts and crafts outlets and some cosy B&Bs. The

Tilba Valley Vineyard (*5km/3 miles north of Tilba Tilba. Old Highway Drive, Narooma. Tel: (03) 4473 7308. www.tilbavalleywines.com*) produces Shiraz, Semillon and Chardonnay wines.

Bega, Mimosa and Bournda

From Tilba, the main road arcs temporarily inland via Bega. If you have a day to spare, an exploration of the coast road through the Bermagui, Tathra and neighbouring national parks of Mimosa Rocks and Bournda is recommended. The small visitor information centre in Bermagui can point you in the right direction (*Lamont St. Tel: (02) 6493 3054*). If you go via Bega, the main attraction is its famous **cheese factory** (*Lagoon St. Tel: (02) 6491 7777. www.begacheese.com.au. Open: 9am–5pm. Free admission*).

Merimbula

Merimbula, 70km (43 miles) north of the Victorian border, serves as the capital of the Sapphire Coast. Surrounded by fine beaches and bisected by its namesake lake, there is plenty to see and do, with Main Beach, south of the lake, being the most popular beach. The lake is a great venue for boating, windsurfing and fishing. The surrounding coast also offers some good diving and cruising with dolphin-watching a speciality. Between September and December, migrating whales also join the party. The visitor information centre provides bookings

(*Beach St. Tel: (02) 6495 1129. www.sapphirecoast.com.au. Open: 9am–4.30pm*). The National Park and Wildlife Service has a Discovery Centre with detailed parks and regional walks information, natural history displays and maps (*Corner of Sapphire Coast and Merimbula Drives. Tel: (02) 6495 5000*).

Eden

Eden is the last coastal settlement before the Victorian Border (47km/ 29 miles away) and has an interesting pioneering and whaling history. Thankfully, chasing the dollar has now turned from killing to simply watching, and several operators offer half-day cruises in season (*Oct–Dec*). For some historical insight, head to the **Killer Whale Museum** (*Imlay St. Tel: (02) 6496 2094. www.killerwhalemuseum.com.au. Open: Mon–Sat 9.15am–3.45pm, Sun 11.15am–3.45pm. Admission charge*). The visitor information centre is

at the main roundabout in town (*Princes Hwy. Tel: (02) 6496 1953. www.sapphirecoast.com.au. Open: daily 9am–5pm*).

Ben Boyd National Park

Ben Boyd National Park is one of the best on the south coast, and although the unsealed roads seem interminable it is worth investigating. The main attractions are Boyd's Tower (a former light station), the 'Pinnacles', an ancient eroded cliff of coloured sands and clay in the northern sector of the park (*2km/1¼ miles from park entrances on Princes Hwy*), and the Green Cape light station (*21km/13 miles from park entrances on Princes Hwy*) in the southern sector. If you have time, the demanding 'Light to Light' track (*30km/19 miles*), which connects the Green Cape light station with Boyd's Tower, passing two campsites along the way, is reputed to be one of the best coastal walks in New South Wales.

The Pinnacles, Ben Boyd National Park

Sunset at Lakes Entrance

VICTORIAN BORDER TO WILSON'S PROMONTORY
Mallacoota

Located over the Victorian border from New South Wales and 23km (14 miles) off the A1, the small coastal resort of Mallacoota is a charming place and quiet outside the holiday season, which for many is part of its appeal. Set alongside the Mallacoota Inlet, which has fine beaches and easy access to the Croajingolong National Park, there are almost unlimited opportunities for coastal walks, bushwalking, wildlife watching, fishing and boating.
For local details tel: (03) 5158 0116. www.visitmallacoota.com.au

Croajingolong National Park

Best known for its remote wild coastline, eucalypt forests, estuaries and heathland, Croajingolong is home to over 1,000 native plants and more than 300 bird species. Largely inaccessible, Point Hicks is one of the few places where you can reach the coast from the A1 (Cann River). Point Hicks was the first land in Australia to be sighted by the crew of Captain Cook's *Endeavour* in 1770 and also hosts mainland Australia's tallest lighthouse, built in 1890.
Tel: 13 1963. www.parkweb.vic.gov.au

Lakes Entrance

Standing where the vast Gippsland Lakes meet the ocean, the once small fishing village of Lakes Entrance has become a popular coastal holiday resort. It is known for its varied coastal scenery, range of accommodation, eateries and water-based activities. The main ocean beach is accessed over the footbridge off the Esplanade and via the Entrance Walking Track (2 hrs). Numerous cruise and fishing charters operate from the esplanade wharf. *Visitor Information Centre. Corner of Marine Parade and The Esplanade. Tel: 1800 637 060. www.discovereastgippsland.com.au*

Gippsland Lakes

The Gippsland Lakes are a series of coastal lakes and inlets surrounding the town of Bairnsdale. With the only road access south of Sale, the Gippsland Lakes Coastal Park is largely inaccessible from Bairnsdale

without a boat. There are some pretty settlements dotted around the margins of the lakes, with Metung particularly picturesque and Paynesville noted for its populations of wild koalas. In Bairnsdale it is worth visiting the **Aboriginal Krowathunkooloong Keeping Place**, which features some moving displays of the brutal Gunnai massacres that took place locally during the 1830s to 1850s (*Dalmahoy St. Tel: (03) 5152 1891. Open: Mon–Fri 9am–5pm. Admission charge*).

From the agricultural service town of Sale you can continue south to Melbourne via Wilson's Promontory National Park and Phillip Island or

Southeast coast: Sydney to Melbourne (2)

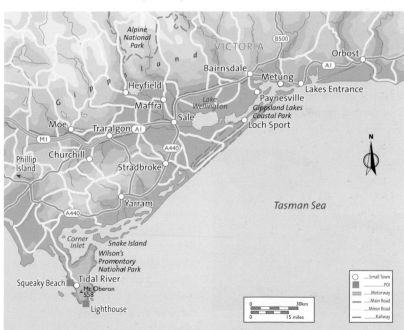

head directly west to Melbourne. Being only half a day's drive away, many visitors save 'The Prom' and Phillip Island for a later date, using Melbourne as a base.

Wilson's Promontory National Park

Wilson's Promontory, 200km (124 miles) from Melbourne, forms the southernmost part of the Australian mainland and contains the largest coastal wilderness area in Victoria. It has been a national park since 1898 and, despite the justified hype surrounding the Great Ocean Road in the state's west, it is without doubt Victoria's best-loved national park.

Known simply as 'The Prom' and with 9,000ha (22,239 acres) set aside as national park, its remote and dramatic coastal aesthetics and abundant wildlife have been a draw for Melbournians for years. Much of the park is only accessible by foot or boat, and even then many of the best tracks take several hours or days to negotiate, so

View over Little Oberon Bay in 'The Prom'

this locks out any real concentration of visitors. However, that said, in Tidal River, an attractive spot in its own right, the only settlement within the park and the main focus for tourism and recreation, it takes a ballot system over the summer to accommodate campers, such is the demand.

The Prom is not a park that can be properly experienced in a day, and a more thorough exploration by foot with two nights' camping or more conventional accommodation around the fringes of the park is recommended. There are many short, day and multi-day walking options available and, provided you are willing to don your walking boots and pack a lunch, you can experience some of the true classics, from the remote 1859 lighthouse (*14.5km/9 miles from Tidal River*) or the iconic view from the park's highest peak, Mount Oberon (*3.4km/2 miles from Tidal River*), to a stroll along the pristine white sands of the aptly named 'squeaky beach' (*2km/1¼ miles from Tidal River*). Here

Dawn breaks over a lagoon at Gippsland Lakes

on The Prom, even a packed lunch can prove an experience as squadrons of beautiful crimson rosellas, amicable wombats and cunning roos all await your convivial acquaintance. If walking is not a possibility, there are still many lovely spots accessible by car. The year 2005 saw two notable events on The Prom: first in summer when wildfires decimated the region; and then, ironically, in August the first snowfalls for years. Thankfully, as usual, the bush has been quick to regenerate.

Tidal River has some 450 camping and caravan sites but there are no powered sites and generators are not permitted. Campfires are also banned, so take a gas or fuel stove. Alternatively, there are self-contained flats and lodges, group lodges, and motor huts with electricity. Note that all this accommodation is very popular and must be booked well in advance. Basic bunk accommodation is also available at the lighthouse but camping is not permitted. Tidal River has a general store, post office, camping gas supplies and a takeaway food shop. Petrol and diesel are available and in summer there is an open-air cinema and a doctor on site.

Park entry admission charge. For detailed information regarding camping and accommodation, phone Parks Victoria. Tel: 131 963/(03) 8627 4700. www.parkweb.vic.gov.au

Boardwalk through the ferns of Lilly Pilly Gully, Wilson's Promontory National Park

Canberra

Alas, poor Canberra (pronounced kaanbrah). Many have not even heard of Australia's capital. Fewer still have heard of the state in which it resides – the Australian Capital Territory, or ACT. And it doesn't end there. The state of New South Wales (that A-list celebrity state that completely surrounds ACT) is over 340 times its size. All in all, it seems like the perfect recipe for chronic low self-esteem. So how did this ever come to pass?

The answer is 'history' or lack of it. There is nothing wrong with Canberra; it is a great place. The problem is that Canberra is less than 100 years old and only has a population of around 350,000. It is, in effect, purpose-built. It all began in 1901 with the official federation of the colonies when Australia was without a national capital. As one might expect, Sydney and Melbourne fought to see who should prevail, but after a fight that lasted more than seven years, the federal government, temporarily based in Melbourne, eventually threw in the towel, called a draw, and decided to create a new territory and a new capital roughly halfway between the two. Once a suitable area of land had been designated, an international competition was initiated to find the right architect for the job of designing the great new capital. The winner, an American called Walter Burley Griffin, had a rather bold design, incorporating a series of geometrical shapes similar to the layouts of Washington, DC and Paris. In 1913, work began and despite a few major setbacks, including Griffin's departure in 1920, the Depression and World War II, the new capital began to take shape. In 1927, the federal politicians sat for the first time in the new (now old) Parliament House and ever since, the city, the capital and the territory (as small and as infant as it is) has gone from strength to strength.

So, when it comes to attractions and aesthetics, Can Berra? Well the answer is a resounding, 'yes', it most certainly can. A visit to the nation's capital will certainly not disappoint and there is plenty to see and do. Unsurprisingly, most of the major attractions are of national significance and surround governance or culture. Here you will find the striking modern façade of the **New Parliament House**, the superb **National Museum of Australia**, or the **National Gallery of Art** all connected by the remarkably efficient and attractive layout that Griffin dutifully

Canberra and the Snowy Mountains

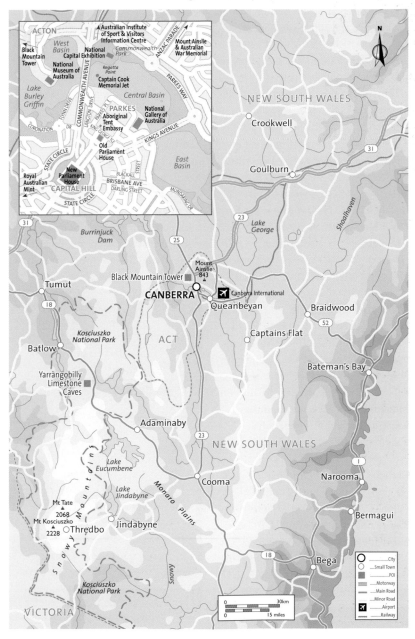

ACTON
Australian Institute of Sport & Visitors Information Centre
West Basin
Black Mountain Tower
National Capital Exhibition
Commonwealth Park
Mount Ainslie & Australian War Memorial
National Museum of Australia
Regatta Point
Captain Cook Memorial Jet
Lake Burley Griffin
Central Basin
PARKES
Aboriginal Tent Embassy
National Gallery of Australia
Old Parliament House
East Basin
Royal Australian Mint
New Parliament House
CAPITAL HILL
BLACKALL STREET
BRISBANE AVE
DARLING STREET
STATE CIRCLE
COMMONWEALTH AVENUE
FLYNN DRIVE
LANGTON DRIVE
HARVEST ST
KING GEORGE TCE
CORONATION DR
KINGS AVENUE
ANZAC PARADE
PARKES WAY
MUNDARING DR

NEW SOUTH WALES

Crookwell

Goulburn

Shoalhaven

31

31

25

23

Lake George

Burrinjuck Dam

Mount Ainslie 843

Black Mountain Tower

CANBERRA

Tumut

18

Canberra International

Queanbeyan

Braidwood

52

Kosciuszko National Park

ACT

Captains Flat

Batlow

Bateman's Bay

Yarrangobilly Limestone Caves

Adaminaby

NEW SOUTH WALES

23

1

Lake Eucumbene

Cooma

Narooma

Lake Jindabyne

Mt Tate 2068

Mt Kosciuszko 2228

Thredbo

Jindabyne

Monaro Plains

Snowy Mountains

Bermagui

Snowy

18

Bega

Kosciuszko National Park

VICTORIA

◯	City
◯	Small Town
◼	POI
	Motorway
	Main Road
	Minor Road
✈	Airport
	Railway

0   30km
0   15 miles

created. At over 500m (1,640ft) above sea level, it can also be refreshingly cool in Canberra and at last you have an Australian city that values its trees. Subsequently, autumn is a great time to visit, when the city is resplendent in golden hue. In winter, the city is a fine base from which to access the Snowy Mountains' ski fields.

The Canberra Visitor Information Centre is 3km (2 miles) north of the city centre. 330 Northbourne Ave. Tel: (02) 6205 0044/1300 554 114. www.visitcanberra. com.au. Open: Mon–Fri 9am–5pm, Sat & Sun 9am–4pm. For general city information, visit www.canberra. citysearch.com.au. For bus information, contact ACTION. Tel: 13 17 10.

The National Triangle

Encompassed within Parkes Way and Lake Burley Griffin to the north, Kings Avenue to the east and Commonwealth Avenue to the west, this area, also known as the Parliamentary Triangle, contains most of the city's and the nation's most important national buildings and cultural institutions.

National Capital Exhibition

Set alongside Lake Burley Griffin, the Capital Exhibition showcases the history of the nation's capital, from its indigenous links to the modern day. Adjacent to the exhibition building, the **Captain Cook Memorial Jet** in the lake bursts into life daily with a 6-tonne spout that exits at over 200kph (124mph) and reaches up to 150m

(492ft). The park is within walking distance of the city centre.
Regatta Point, Commonwealth Park, Parkes. Tel: (02) 6247 1068. www.nationalcapital.gov.au. Open: Mon–Fri 9am–5pm, Sat & Sun 10am–4pm. Free admission; charge for tours.

National Gallery of Australia

Usually the first to host the most significant national and international travelling exhibitions, the gallery's cavernous halls have an impressive collection of works and a wide range of media, from the ancient dot paintings of the Aboriginals to state-of-the-art works using the latest digital video

The entrance to New Parliament House, Canberra

The Old Parliament House was once the political hub of the nation

techniques. Don't miss the sculpture garden outside.

Parkes Pl, Parkes. Tel: (02) 6240 6411. www.nga.gov.au. Open: 9am–5pm. Free admission; charge for travelling exhibitions. Buses: 31, 34, 36 & 39.

New Parliament House

Once described by travel writer Bill Bryson as resembling a huge Christmas tree stand, the New Parliament House, completed in 1988, is the architectural showpiece of Canberra. Although hardly in the same league as Sydney's

Opera House and Harbour Bridge, it is still intriguing and instantly recognisable. Where else in the world is there a building that has a well-groomed lawn as a roof and where you could once (in effect) walk all over a nation's politicians? Sadly, given the massive increase in security since 11 September 2001, you can no longer do so, but under watchful eyes you can turn your attentions to the impressive interior. There – politicians aside – you can muse upon various treasures including Arthur Boyd's impressive

Shoalhaven Tapestry. When Parliament is in session, access is allowed to 'Question Time' in the House of Representatives (*2pm. Tickets free*). *Capital Hill. Tel: (02) 6277 5399. www.aph.gov.au. Open: 9am–5pm; guided tours 9am–4pm. Free parking available. Buses: 31, 34, 36 & 39.*

Old Parliament House

In the heart of the National Triangle and completed in 1927, this was the most important building in the capital and its raison d'être. It was the hub of the nation's complex political life for over 60 years before the more imposing New Parliament House replaced it. As

Avenue of Flags in the Parliamentary Triangle

well as housing the **National Portrait Gallery**, it serves as a political museum. Immediately outside the Old Parliament building is the unofficial **Aboriginal Tent Embassy**, an ongoing Aboriginal protest. In many ways it speaks for itself and serves as a pertinent reminder that the Aboriginal people of Australia lived a successful sustainable existence for tens of thousands of years before any European system of governance or the concept of politics was ever created, let alone forced upon them.

King George Terrace, Parkes. Tel: (02) 6270 8222. www.oph.gov.au. Open: 9am–5pm. Admission charge. Buses: 31, 34, 36 & 39.

Outside the Triangle
Australian Institute of Sport

Opened in 1981 to provide training facilities for Australia's elite, visitors are given the opportunity to join a resident athlete on a 90-minute tour to view aspects of the nation's sporting history and to see some of the champions or 'wannabes' in action. You can also try your hand at various sports including rowing and golf.

Leverrier Cres, Bruce. Tel: (02) 6214 1010. www.ausport.gov.au. Tours: Mon–Fri 10am/11.30am/1pm/2.30pm. Admission charge.

Australian War Memorial and Anzac Parade

Sitting below Mount Ainslie, the Australian War Memorial encompasses a large, well-presented museum and some dramatic perspectives. For many, other than the sheer mood of the place, the 'Peacekeeping' display will appeal along with 'G-For George', one of the few remaining Lancaster bombers. Children are well catered for in the interactive Discovery Zone.

Treloar Cres (top of Anzac Parade), Campbell. Tel: (02) 6243 4211. www.awm.gov.au. Open: 10am–5pm. Free admission. Buses: 33 & 40.

City lookouts

A fine start to any exploration of the city is one or more of the excellent lookouts close to the city centre. This will give you an impression of the orderly perspectives and the layout of the city as a whole. Most prominent is the 195m (640ft) **Black Mountain Tower** to the west of the city centre. Like some jagged hypodermic, it is hardly a beautiful sight, but the views are worth seeing. There are three public viewing areas as well as a restaurant and an exhibition, 'Making Connections', which showcases the history of Australian telecommunications (*Black Mountain Dr, Acton. Tel: 1800 806 718. www.blackmountaintower.com.au. Restaurant tel: (02) 6247 5518. Open: 9am–10pm. Admission charge*). Superb perspectives of the Anzac Parade and the old and new parliament buildings are on offer from the 843m (2,766ft) summit of **Mount Ainslie**, east of the city centre (*Fairbairn Avenue to Mount Ainslie Drive*).

National Museum of Australia

In tune with most national museums, this is an exciting state-of-the-art institution. Sitting proudly on the shores of Lake Burley Griffin, it offers a fine range of exciting displays and themed galleries showcasing the nation's developing identity and just about everything conceivably 'Aussie' from the in-depth issues of indigenous Australia, sport and natural history to the more quirky aspects like the country's inexplicable inventory of 'Big Things'. This museum requires at least a whole day and you should arrange something completely banal before and after your visit or your head might explode.

Lawson Cres, Acton. Tel: 1800 026 132. www.nma.gov.au. Open: 9am–5pm. Free admission; charge to some specialist and travelling displays. Buses: 3, 934 & 981.

Royal Australian Mint

While the prospect of visiting a factory that can spew out more money in a minute than most earn in a year may seem a little masochistic, a trip to the Australian mint can still prove entertaining. You can view the minting process and then learn about the history of Australian currency, its production and design. The mint's coin collection is also impressive and you can mint your very own AU$1 coin.

Denison St, Deakin. Tel: (02) 6202 6800. www.ramint.gov.au. Open: Mon–Fri 9am–4pm, Sat & Sun 10am–4pm. Free admission.

View towards Mount Kosciuszko in spring

The Snowy Mountains

The very title seems incongruous for Australia, and it is certainly contrary to the overseas image of bronzed surfers and koalas. Yet here, on the highest elevations of the Great Dividing Range, it does snow, you can ski and snowmen can retain their obligatory smiley faces long after sun-up. Indeed, here at Charlotte Pass in 1994 Australia's lowest temperature was recorded at an icy –24°C (–11.2°F).

The Snowy Mountains is a loose term that describes the ranges within the Kosciuszko (pronounced kozzie-usko) National Park, the Snowy River National Park and the Alpine National Park. At almost 7,000sq km (2,702sq miles), Kosciuszko is the largest of the three, extending from the border of the Australian Capital Territory to the Victorian border, and within it is the nation's highest peak, Mount Kosciuszko (2,228m/7,310ft).

However, remember this is Australia and although the peaks are Alpine and contain an impressive milieu of rugged mountains and wilderness, they are decidedly non-peaky in the classic sense. Yet the region is still aesthetically pleasing in both winter and summer, which makes it popular with recreational skiers and bushwalkers.

The Snowy River originates in the park and flows south to Victoria where it joins the mighty Murray, part of Australia's longest combined river system, the Murray–Darling. The Snowy River has been heavily utilised for power generation, with many tunnels and dams making up the Snowy Mountains Scheme hydroelectric system, reputedly one of the most complex integrated water and hydroelectric power schemes in the world.

A visit to the area generally revolves around three main activities: skiing

Melbourne and central Victoria

Victoria is mainland Australia's smallest and most densely populated state, with the undisputed star of urbanity being Melbourne, its capital, which – so typical of Australian cities – around 70 per cent of the state's 5.2 million people call home. First settled by European farmers in the 1830s, the discovery of gold in 1851 for a while transformed the fortunes of the region.

From the solid roots provided by the precious metal, a thriving, truly cosmopolitan city grew. The visitor now journeying on a bus or a train, confronted by so many nationalities, would be forgiven for wondering in which country they were. And the contrasts do not end there. Victoria has one of the most diverse geographies of all the states with mountain ranges bedecked with snow in winter, fertile coastal plains, some lush, some parched, and in the far northwest sun-baked desert largely devoid of humanity. There is even a river running through it – the Yarra – that lays its muddy waters to rest in Port Phillip Bay after slipping under the shadow of Melbourne's lofty, glistening high-rises. Then there is the weather, Melbourne's notorious 'four seasons in one day' weather. On a summer's day in Melbourne, with a wind change it can be 40°C (104°F) in the morning and 15°C (59°F) in the afternoon; the city can see no rain for weeks then receive a

thunderous downfall; and in winter the streets can be like Scotland in mid-February. Little wonder many materialistic Melbournians dream of that second home on the Gold Coast.

For the visitor, Melbourne and central Victoria offer plenty to see and do, even if you are still recovering from the inevitable 'wow' effect of Sydney. Sydney's stunning natural harbour ensures that Melbourne could never be so pretty, but venture beyond suburbia to the Dandenongs, the Mornington Peninsula or Daylesford's Spa Country and you will find that the region has beaches, bush and character on a par with anything in New South Wales.

Melbourne is also the events capital of Australia, especially when it comes to sport. This is the home of the annual Australian Grand Prix, the Australian Tennis Open, the Melbourne Cup horse race and that all-Aussie event the Australian Rules Football (AFL) Final.

You can also get that wonderful wildlife fix in Victoria. Here you

(June–Oct); bushwalking in summer; and sightseeing, particularly scenic drives year-round.

Although **Cooma**, in the Monaro Plains (*114km/71 miles south of Canberra*), is often considered the capital of the 'Snowies', it is the mainly winter resort of **Jindabyne** (*176km/ 109 miles from Canberra*) on the eastern fringe of the national park that hosts the bulk of tourist traffic. The two main ski fields are at **Perisher Blue** (*33km/ 20 miles from Jindabyne*) and **Thredbo** (*34km/21 miles from Jindabyne*). Thredbo is considered Australia's best Alpine resort and has a full range of winter accommodation and amenities. In spring and summer, the National Park and Wildlife Service promotes summer activities, with alpine flowers being a popular attraction. Mountain biking and horse trekking are also in demand. If climbing Mount Kosciuszko appeals, it is considered a day walk of medium difficulty in summer and starting points are at Charlotte Pass (via Perisher Blue, 12.5km/8 miles,

4½ hours, one-way) or Thredbo (via the chairlift, 6.5km/4 miles, 2½ hours, one-way).

The Alpine Way (103km/64 miles) from Khancoban to Jindabyne is considered the best scenic drive in the region. Other attractions within the park include trout fishing around Adaminaby and the Yarrangobilly Limestone Caves (*On SH18 northwest of Cooma*).

Jindabyne is accessed via SH23 and Cooma, 176km (109 miles) south of Canberra.

The National Park and Wildlife Service Snowy Region Visitors Centre is east of the main shopping centre in Jindabyne, off Kosciuszko Rd. Tel: 1800 004 439. www.snowymountains.com.au. Open: 8.30am–5pm. Staff provide national parks & up-to-date weather information, sell detailed maps & issue park day-use & camping permits. Day vehicle access admission charge. For ski information, visit www.perisherblue.com.au & www.thredbo.com.au

Rocky Tors draped in snowdrifts, Mount Kosciuszko National Park

can encounter everything from fruit bats to penguins and, of course, the ubiquitous koala (don't you dare call it a bear!). There are the vineyards of the Yarra and Mornington to tour, and if you need a day cooling the wallet you can always resort to a spot of simple nationality watching under the sun (or umbrella) in Federation Square.

Melbourne

Given the relatively compact nature of Victoria (by Australian standards, that is), Melbourne is the ideal base from which to explore most of the state before continuing on the Great Ocean Road to Adelaide and beyond, or embarking on a trip to Tasmania. Provided the weather is kind, a few days should suffice for the main attractions

Central Victoria (*see p76 for orange tour route; p80 for purple drive route*)

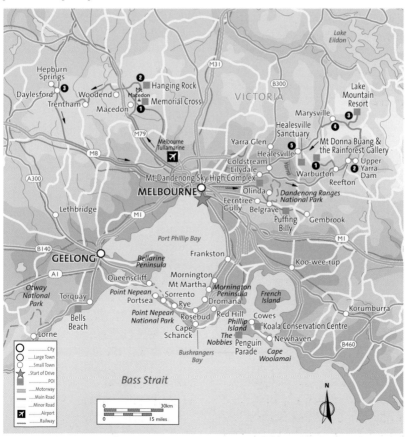

Melbourne and central Victoria

MELBOURNE TRAVEL PASSES

Sadly, despite the character of Melbourne's iconic trams, the city's rail and tram network (particularly the trains) has a bad reputation for service, with frequent cancellations and delays. However, as a visitor and not a commuter this should not ruin your stay or stop you from utilising the various tickets and pass systems.

One Metcard ticket covers trams, buses and trains over two metropolitan zones. Zone 1 covers the city centre, while Zone 2 reaches the city fringes. There are city saver, 2-hour, Sunday saver, daily, weekly and monthly tickets available (with further savings possible on 2, 5 and 10 multiple tickets of the 2-hour, daily and city savers). Tickets are available at all train stations (tellers and machines) and on ticket machines on most trams. Generally speaking, a daily ticket in Zone 1 will suffice. For details, *tel: 131 638*. *www.metlinkmelbourne.com.au*

the third-largest tram network in the world. A single Metcard fare system covers trains, trams and buses, and the city operates a system of saver cards. Three zones cover greater Melbourne, but you will rarely need anything other than a day Zone 1 ticket as this covers everything within about 10km (6 miles) of the city centre (*see left*). The **Met Shop** has useful maps of tram, bus and train routes and timetables (*103 Swanston St. Open: Mon–Fri 8.30am–5.30pm, Sat 9am–1pm). For train, bus and tram information, tel: 131 638. www.metlinkmelbourne.com.au & www.viclink.com.au*

Eureka Tower and Skydeck

Completed in mid-2006 and standing at a height of 253m (830ft), Eureka Tower is Melbourne's tallest building and a fine place to start your explorations of the city – for the view anyway. There is an impressive observation deck on the 88th floor but the added attraction is 'The Edge', a see-through glass box that extends from the building's façade. Additional touches include walls that begin opaque and then gradually clear, and soothing music that turns into the sound of grinding metal and breaking glass. *Riverside Quay, Southbank. Tel: (03) 9693 8888. www.eurekaskydeck.com.au. Open: 10am–10pm. Admission charge ('The Edge' additional). Train & tram: Flinders Street Station; footbridge across the Yarra River.*

within the city before looking beyond the suburbs.

A good starting point is the view from the lofty Eureka Tower then back down to earth in Federation Square or St Kilda. If you can, take a walk along the Yarra to the newly developed Docklands (*see p68*), or through one of the city centre's gracious garden parks. Then there is shopping in the Central Business District and an all too brief sampling of the city's many quality and cosmopolitan restaurants and cafés.

Also worth mentioning are Melbourne's iconic trams that are a convenient and relatively cheap way to get around. They have been a feature of the city since 1885, and the city hosts

Melbourne city centre
(see p68 for orange walk route)

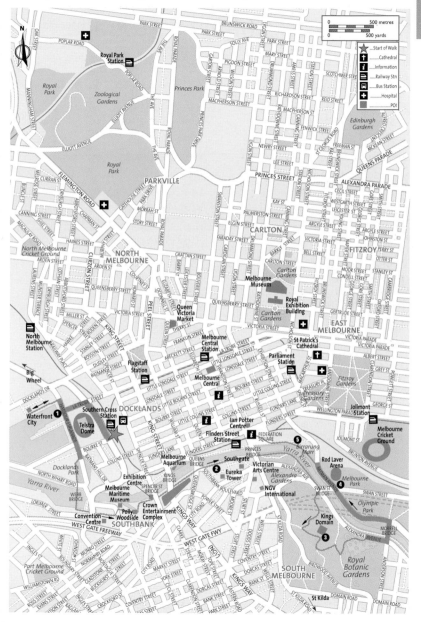

Melbourne:
events capital of Australia

Though Sydneysiders would vehemently disagree, Melbourne is the undisputed events capital of Australia. Why that should be the case is debatable, but one thing is for sure, it is nothing new. In Carlton Gardens, near the heart of Melbourne's Central Business District and in stark contrast to the glistening high-rises that cast their shadows upon it, is the Royal Exhibition Building, completed in 1880. It was commissioned for the Melbourne International Exhibition, one of the most significant events of its time, and is now a World Heritage Site. The city's latest event venues include the mighty Melbourne Cricket Ground (MCG), Telstra Dome with its

The Melbourne Cup is hugely popular

retractable roof, and the ultra-modern façades of Federation Square.

The big six

The big six annual events in Melbourne are: the Australian Tennis Open (January); the Moomba Waterfest (March); the Australian Grand Prix (March); the Australian Rules Football (AFL) Grand Final (September); the Spring Carnival (Melbourne Cup) (November); and the Boxing Day cricket test match. There are dozens more, some big events in their own right, like the Commonwealth Games in 2006, but the big six are the traditional giants of the annual sports and social calendar.

The city is proud to hold the **Australian Tennis Open** at the Rod Laver Arena adjacent to the MCG, and the home crowd becomes especially fired up when an Australian has a chance of taking the title.

The **Moomba Waterfest** is one of the longest-running festivals in Australia, having originated in 1955. There is a procession of floats and various, mainly water-based, events staged on and around the Yarra River. The **Grand Prix** is much loved,

Celebrating the Grand Prix with a beer or two

especially by the corporate set, and is held at a permanent circuit in Albert Park.

The **AFL Grand Final** is a huge event and staged at the MCG. AFL is a complex sport, arguably the most Australian, and massively popular. In 2009, it was the Geelong Cats who won in their third final appearance in a row.

Of all the events, the **Spring Carnival** is the most 'Melbourne'. Held at the Flemington Racecourse, this is one of the most important horse-racing events in the world, with the Melbourne Cup – dubbed 'the race that stops a nation' – the main event, and an extrovert display of high fashion and social excess. It attracts huge crowds over the four race days, with the Oaks Race Day, also known as 'Ladies Day', the main day to strut your designer stuff.

The **Boxing Day test match** is another Melbourne favourite, when the worshipped national team takes on whichever poor nation happens to be on tour that year.

Other annual events in Melbourne include: the Melbourne Food and Wine Festival (March); Melbourne International Flower and Garden Festival (March); the Comedy Festival (April); Writers' Festival (August); Fringe Festival (September); and the Melbourne Festival (October). And the quirkiest? Perhaps the annual Rubber Duck Race on the Yarra on **Australia Day** (26 January) or the day during the Fringe Festival of 2001, when over 4,000 Melbournians took their clothes off and posed nude along the bank of the Yarra for artist/photographer Spencer Tunick. No worries, mate!

Federation Square

Initiated as an international architectural design competition in 1996, and opened in 2002 at a cost of AU$450 million, Fed Square (as it is known) is one of the most ambitious construction projects ever undertaken in Australia and Melbourne's answer to the Guggenheim Museum in Bilbao or the Pompidou in Paris. Covering an entire block, it is an intriguing and – for most – attractive combination of angular steel girders and plate-glass caverns that subtly houses restaurants, cafés, performance spaces, the visitor information centre, **Australian Racing Museum** and the **Ian Potter Centre** (*National Gallery of Victoria, see below*). It has become the main focus for visitors to Melbourne and you will find yourself returning time and again.
Corner of Flinders St and St Kilda Rd. www.federationsquare.com.au. Train & tram: Flinders Street Station.
Visitor Information Centre. Corner of Flinders & Swanston Sts. Tel: (03) 9658 9658. www.thatsmelbourne.com.au/ touristinformation. Open: 9am–6pm.

Melbourne Cricket Ground (The MCG)

Regarded more as a cathedral than a stadium, the hallowed turf of the MCG (or 'The G' as it is known) has hosted countless historic cricket matches and Aussie Rules Football games as well as the 1956 Olympics, rock concerts and, most recently, the Commonwealth Games in 2006. Tours take in the

National Sports Museum, the **Australian Cricket Hall of Fame**, and exhibitions on Aussie Rules.
Jolimont St. Tel: (03) 9657 8879. www.mcg.org.au. Open: 9.30am–4.30pm; tours 10am–3pm on non-event days. Tram & train: Jolimont.

Melbourne Museum and Carlton Gardens

Set alongside the Royal Exhibition Building (*see p64*), the Melbourne Museum could hardly be more striking, and the interior and art exhibits will not disappoint. The Bunjilaka Aboriginal Centre and 'Koorie Voices' displays combine in an Aboriginal presentation, while elsewhere there are natural history, science and culture displays.
Carlton Gardens. Tel: 131 102. www.museumvictoria.com.au. Open: 10am–5pm daily. Admission charge for adults. Tram: Carlton Gardens.

National Gallery of Victoria

Given the city's prosperous past, the indigenous and non-indigenous collections of this gallery are

The striking façade of Melbourne Museum

particularly impressive, especially the 19th-century European art purchased during Melbourne's boom period. The repository is housed in two venues: the Ian Potter Centre (NGV Australia), and the NGV International.

NGV Ian Potter, Federation Square. NGV International, 180 St Kilda Rd. Tel: (03) 8620 2222. www.ngv.vic.gov.au. Open: 10am–5pm. Free admission; charge for visiting exhibitions. Train: Flinders Street Station.

The Royal Exhibition Building

Queen Victoria Market and Melbourne Central

The iconic Victoria Street Market has expanded since the 1870s, and has a historic meat hall and the dairy hall, which includes nearly 40 delicatessen stalls. The sheds opposite hold mass-market kitsch and Australiana, but the food sections are worth a look.

Nearby is the far more modern Melbourne Central shopping mall, surrounding and incorporating the old 1890 50m (164ft) **Shot Tower**.

Queen Victoria Market, 513 Elizabeth Street. Tel: (03) 9320 5822. www.qvm.com.au. Open: Tue & Thur 6am–2pm, Fri 6am–6pm, Sat 6am–3pm, Sun 9am–4pm; tours available.

St Kilda

St Kilda, on the shores of the tranquil Port Phillip Bay, is the city's best-known suburb and to Melbourne what Bondi is to Sydney – without the surf, the pretension and the stunning swathe of golden sand. For wild ocean beaches you must venture further to the Mornington Peninsula and Surf coasts. A lack of pounding surf aside, the attractive waterfront, historic pier, iconic Luna Park funfair and the happening, alternative street life of Acland Street and Fitzroy Street in St Kilda more than make up for it.

Tram: St Kilda Rd.

Southbank

The 'Southbank' of the Yarra River forms the heart of the cultural and entertainment precinct of the city, much of it taken up by the vast **Crown Entertainment Complex**, home to the Crown Casino and its various adjuncts, including several hotels, a cinema, restaurants, bars and nightclubs, and boutiques. To the west, the main attraction is the tall ship *Polly Woodside*, built in 1885 (*Tel: (03) 9656 9800. www.pollywoodside.com.au*). To the east, the **Victorian Arts Centre** dominates, and plans are afoot for its expansion and redevelopment (*Tel: 1300 182 183. www.theartscentre.com.au. Train: Flinders Street Station*).

Walk: Along the River Yarra

Like so many city rivers, the Yarra is hardly a model of clarity and cleanliness, but it remains the dominant feature of the Central Business District, and many high-profile attractions grace its meandering banks. From the intriguing façades of Federation Square to the quiet Botanic Gardens, a walk along the River Yarra offers many delights. See page 63 for map.

This walk is about 7km (4 miles). Allow a whole day.

From Southern Cross Station, head northwest exiting onto the Telstra Dome pedestrian walkway. Head towards the Telstra Dome and to the Waterfront, turn right then left to Waterfront City.

From Waterfront City, return past the stadium and along Harbour Esplanade, through Docklands Park to the Webb (pedestrian) Bridge. Having crossed the Yarra bridge, head east (left) along the riverbank.

1 Docklands

Fringed by the space-age-looking Southern Cross Station and dominated by the Telstra Stadium, the Docklands is currently the pride of Melbourne's progressive inner-city redevelopment programme, and its expansion continues apace in Waterfront City. Over the last decade, the former derelict docks have changed into an intriguing milieu of apartment and office blocks, marina, parklands, classy restaurants and landscaped open spaces replete with outlandish urban

sculptures and the new 'big wheel'. All in all, love it or hate it, welcome to modern Australian city living. Besides, where else on earth would you see a square cow up a tree?

The River Yarra attracts many rowers

2 Southbank

From west to east are the new
Convention Centre, the tall ship
Polly Woodside, the Exhibition Centre,
Crown Entertainment Complex
(home to the casino) and the
Southgate shopping arcade. There is
always plenty to see here, from
simple people-watching to buskers.
If you have time, the **Melbourne
Aquarium** on the opposite bank may
appeal (*via the Kings Bridge. Tel: (03)
9923 5999. www.melbourneaquarium.
com.au. Open: 9.30am–6pm.
Admission charge*).

For a light lunch, there are plenty
of eateries around, with the main food
hall being at Southgate (*near
Princes Bridge*).
*From Southgate, pass under the Princes
Bridge and continue east.*

3 The Gardens and Kings Domain

This section of the riverbank plays host
to the Alexandra Gardens with their
historic boatsheds. If you are lucky, the
various rowing clubs will be out on
the river practising (try very early
in the morning or at weekends).
Beyond Alexandra Gardens and the
Swan Street Bridge (1952) is the Kings
Domain and Royal Botanic Gardens.
The ornamental lake at the far
northwestern corner of the Botanic
Gardens is of particular note.
*From the ornamental lakes, head across
the Yarra River on the 1899 Morrell
Bridge (pedestrian only). Then head back
west along the riverbank.*

An intriguing façade in Federation Square

4 Melbourne Park

East of the Swan Street Bridge is
Melbourne Park which, along with
Yarra Park (home of Melbourne Cricket
Ground), contains the city's principal
sporting venues. The Rod Laver Arena
hosts the Australian Tennis Open and
the occasional rock concert.
Continue west along the riverbank.

5 Birrarung Marr

Birrarung Marr (Birrarung means
'River of Mists' and 'Marr' means 'side
of the river') is one of the city's newest
parks. Amid its stunning aesthetics are
the 39 Federation Bells that play seven
brief compositions twice daily at 8am
and 5pm. Also note the stunning
installation *Angel* beside the river by
Melbourne artist Deborah Halpern.
*From Birrarung Marr Park you can end
your walk at Federation Square and
access tram or trains at the Flinders
Street Station.*

Walk: Along the River Yarra

The Dandenongs

The 3,200ha (7,907-acre) Dandenong Ranges National Park lies at the eastern fringe of suburban Melbourne. The ranges are like some mini, green Uluru on the edge of the vast city sprawl, and reach a height of 600m (1,968ft). Due to the elevation, they have acted as an oasis of green and cool retreat for Melbournians for over 150 years. In winter, it can even snow here. To enter the world of the Dandenongs is like exploring one huge botanic garden. Instantly, all sense of city disappears and the sense of relief is palpable.

The ranges are best explored on foot and by car. They stretch from Ferntree Gully in the southwest to Montrose in the north, and east to the fringes of the Yarra Valley. There are several small villages at the higher elevations, best accessed by winding minor roads from Ferntree Gully or Belgrave. **Olinda**, in the heart of the park, is arguably the prettiest and certainly the most tourist-oriented. However, the ranges' best assets have little to do with anything human-made and everything to do with things that grow. The Dandenongs is all about its forested protected areas, wildlife, walks and formal gardens.

There are numerous picnic grounds and many short walks; under the towering Mountain Ash forest of Sherbrooke (the largest section of the park) **Grants Picnic Ground** is a firm favourite. Here, rapacious and noisy flocks of birds descend, particularly late in the day when the area becomes abuzz with 'bird-meets-sandwich'

Welcome to
**Dandenong Ranges
National Park**
Home of tall trees, fern gullies and native wildlife

Two cheeky cockatoos welcome visitors to Dandenong Ranges National Park (bird food is sold in the café). Beyond the avian mayhem, the short walks (ranging from 300m/330yds to 7km/4 miles) are another attraction.

Of the formal gardens, the 40ha (99-acre) **National Rhododendron Gardens** offer more then the usual spectacular displays of colour when 15,000 of their mainstay bloom from September to November. A rock garden, lake, fern gully, camellia garden and Japanese Cherry Walk all feature amid mature exotic trees, flowering shrubs and, in spring, over 250,000 bulbs (*From Olinda–Monbulk Rd (off the Georgian Rd), Olinda. Open: 10am–5pm. Admission charge*).

Other gardens worth exploring include the 13ha (32-acre) **Alfred Nicholas Gardens** (*Sherbrooke Rd, via Kallista. Admission charge*), the 2.4ha (6-acre) **George Tindale Garden** (*Sherbrooke Rd, via Kallista. Admission charge*), and the **William Ricketts Sanctuary**, with its attractive Aboriginal-oriented sculpture garden (*Mount Dandenong Tourist Dr, north of Olinda. Open: 10am–4.30pm. Admission charge*).

For the best views in the park, head to the **Mount Dandenong Sky High Complex**. At 600m (1,968ft), it is the highest point and the best view within the city boundary; on a clear day, particularly at sunset, it is superb. The grounds feature an English garden and a maze (*26 Observatory Rd, Mount Dandenong. Tel: (03) 9751 0443. www.skyhighmtdandenong.com.au*).

The park is an excellent venue for picnics

Although not strictly within the park, another attraction in the area is the steam train affectionately dubbed **Puffing Billy**. It runs between Belgrave and Gembrook, taking in the Emerald Lake, a very pleasant park and a great picnic spot (*Tel: (03) 9757 0700. www.puffingbilly.com.au. Admission charge. City train to Belgrave, then Puffing Billy from Puffing Billy Station Belgrave or Bus: 695 (weekdays, Belgrave to Gembrook), tel: 131 638*).

Dandenongs National Park, Visitor Information Centre. 1211 Burwood Hwy, Upper Ferntree Gully. Tel: (03) 9758 7522. www.parkweb.vic.gov.au. www.dandenongrangestourism.com.au

Mornington Peninsula

At 50km (31 miles) from Melbourne, the Mornington Peninsula is Melbourne's most accessible holiday destination and a 'backyard' that would be the envy of any city. It is a well-kept secret, and it seems that only Melbournians are aware of its inherent delights.

Part of the allure is the coastal environment, where the Mornington excels. On one side of the peninsula there are wild ocean beaches backed by 25ha (62 acres) of undisturbed national park, while on the other side are the more sheltered, shallow beaches of Port Phillip Bay. The 'bayside' beaches are famous for their iconic, colourful beach boxes, which have become a symbol for the region. Combined, these contrasting environments offer the perfect aquatic playground. Add to that some of the best wineries in the state, a rash of golf courses, some excellent art galleries, walks and picnic sites and all you need is a sunny day.

Colourful beach boxes, Mornington Peninsula

The Mornington really begins beyond Frankston, considered the last true connected suburb of the city. From there, by taking the coast road, you can access some of the best of the bayside beaches at Mornington or **Mount Martha**.

Before heading out on the peninsula proper, take in the views from its highest point, the 303m (994ft) **Arthur's Seat**, named after the dormant volcanic plug in Edinburgh, Scotland (*Summit road signposted off the Nepean Hwy at Dromana*). On a clear day, the whole western section of the peninsula is laid out before you, and to the north you may be able to see the high-rises of the city over 80km (50 miles) away. There are some pleasant walks near the summit, particularly from the **Seawinds Gardens** nearby.

Bayside, from Arthur's Seat, the communities of **Dromana**, **Rosebud** and **Rye** stretch towards **Sorrento** and **Portsea**, two of the most exclusive postcodes in Victoria and where the bayside and ocean beaches are almost within walking distance of each other. Sorrento and Portsea have some of the best amenities and ambience.

A vehicular ferry connects Sorrento with **Queenscliff** on the Bellarine Peninsula. Encompassing the tip of the Mornington Peninsula, **Point Nepean National Park** is a nationally important site containing the remains of military fortifications from the 1880s, and World Wars I and II. Point Nepean itself is 7km (4 miles) from the park entrance and is accessed by foot, bike, or by scheduled transporter (*Tel: (03) 5984 4276. www.parkweb.vic.gov.au. Admission charge*).

The ocean side of the peninsula is largely reserved as national park and has some stunning surf beaches. The back beach at Sorrento is a state classic, but to escape the crowds try **Koonya Beach** further east (*via Hughes Rd, Blairgowrie. Vehicle access in summer. Admission charge*).

Further east is **Cape Schanck**, and the clifftop walk to the beach at **Bushrangers Bay** (3km/2 miles) is considered one of the best walks in the region. Inland from Cape Schanck there are over 100 vineyards, with most centred on the small community of **Red Hill**.

The visitor information centre at Dromana provides maps and general details. 359B Point Nepean Rd, Dromana. Tel: (03) 5987 3078. www.visitmorningtonpeninsula.org

Melbourne and central Victoria

Sorrento Back Beach, typical of the Mornington Peninsula's superb ocean beaches

Phillip Island

Phillip Island is considered one of Australia's primary ecotourism destinations, attracting over 1.6 million visitors a year – quite impressive when you consider the island is only 26km long and 9km wide (16 by 6 miles). So what's the appeal? Much of it no doubt lies in its coastal scenery and its beaches, and then there is the Motorcycle Grand Prix racing circuit, its fur seal colony and the copious wild koalas. However, the star attractions are the hopelessly cute little penguins at the celebrated 'Penguin Parade'.

140km (87 miles) from Melbourne.

Penguin Parade and The Nobbies

For many, the concept of seeing a penguin in the wild is irresistible, and Phillip Island has one of the largest breeding colonies of Little Blue Penguins in Australia. The Little Blues are the smallest of the penguin species, and they do not need cold water or ice underneath their little 'happy feet'. The penguins come ashore at night to roost in their burrows and feed their chicks. Up to 40 can be viewed from purpose-built platforms, or at closer range should you wish to part with more cash *(Ventnor Rd, Summerlands. Tel: (03) 5951 2800. www.penguins.org.au.*

Woolamai surf beach

Open: daily at dusk. Admission charge. Book ahead).

At the tip of the peninsula, overlooking the seal colony, is the new Nobbies Centre. The centre has an impressive range of facilities and interpretive displays, including live webcams of the seal colony. Penguins can be seen during the day below the boardwalks and there are various clifftop viewpoints (*Ventnor Rd, Summerlands. Tel: (03) 5951 2800. www.penguins.org. au. Open: 10am–dusk. Free admission).*

Cowes and koalas

Cowes is Phillip Island's largest community and its most popular holiday location. The beaches are well sheltered, gently sloping, and among the safest on the island. The **pier**, built in 1870, receives plenty of attention and serves as the staging point for the Cowes to Stony Point passenger ferry and also for **scenic cruises** to view the seal colonies of The Nobbies and French Island. Cowes is named after the coastal town on the Isle of Wight in England.

A few kilometres south of Cowes is the **Koala Conservation Centre**. The island has a healthy wild population, but this is the best place to get up close and personal (*Phillip Island Rd. Tel: (03) 5951 2800. www.penguins.org.au. Open: 10am–dusk. Admission charge).*

Other attractions

The **Motorcycle Grand Prix circuit** hosts major international events and

Enjoying the shade along the waterfront at Cowes

is open to the public for tours and circuits in V8 racing cars (*Back Beach Rd. Tel: (03) 5952 2710. www.phillipislandcircuit.com.au. Charges for tours).*

Cape Woolamai has the best surf beach on the island, some fine coastal walks and good views of the island from its highest point. There is also a large colony of Short-tailed Shearwaters that, like the penguins, return at night to their burrows but with much less style and attention.

The principal visitor information centre on the island is located over the bridge in Newhaven. Main Rd. Tel: (03) 5956 7447. www.visitphillipisland.com

Melbourne and central Victoria

Tour: The Mount Macedon Ranges and Spa Country

Less than a 2-hour drive northwest of Melbourne, this region offers some of the best of rural Victoria. From the expansive views atop Mount Macedon and an exploration of the legendary picnic site, Hanging Rock, head west to the arty township of Daylesford. See page 61 for map.

Allow at least a whole day. Total distance 225km (140 miles).

From the centre of Melbourne, head west via the West Gate Bridge and Western Ring Rd to the Calder Hwy (M79). Exit the freeway at Mount Macedon taking Mt Macedon Rd. Climb the mountain, taking a left turn along Cameron Drive to Mount Macedon (56km/35 miles total).

1 Mount Macedon

Any 'mount' will attract people to climb it, but stick a large memorial cross near the 1,010m (3,314ft) summit and it is sure to have the masses heading 'heavenwards'. The 21m (69ft) Memorial Cross crowning the southern flank of Mount Macedon was erected in the 1930s and over the years has survived lightning strikes and fire. It remains an abiding site of reverence, not to mention offering some memorable views south as far as Melbourne and the Dandenongs. There is a picnic site beside the main car park as well as a visitor centre and tearooms. Back at the start of Cameron Drive it is worth taking the short (but steep) walk

to the Camel's Hump to see the views north to Hanging Rock and beyond. *Back on Mt Macedon Rd, turn left and descend the mount following signs (and by sight) to Hanging Rock (6km/4 miles).*

2 Hanging Rock

Hanging Rock is the most famous – or infamous – picnic site in Victoria. The name refers to just one of the remarkable rock formations that is the eroded remains of a 'mamelon', a particular kind of volcanic lava. Other features with names like

The memorial cross on Mount Macedon

Hanging Rock is a remarkable rock formation that is great fun to explore

Stonehenge, Flying Saucer, Letterbox and The Eagle reach a height of 105m (344ft), securing fine views across the surrounding countryside. The mount is rich in wildlife, with the occasional koala in evidence, and there is a good Discovery Centre, café and picnic facilities. As for the infamy and 'that' notorious picnic? Well, all will be revealed where you get there!
South Rock Rd. Tel: (03) 5427 0295. Open: summer 9am–6pm; winter 9am–5pm. Admission charge.
From Hanging Rock, proceed to Woodend via South Rock Rd (Woodend-Romsey Rd). From the centre of Woodend, take the Daylesford Rd (west, via Trentham, signposted, 38km/24 miles).

3 Daylesford and Hepburn Springs

For many years, Daylesford (and its near neighbour Hepburn Springs) has been one of the state's most popular weekend or day-trip destinations.

Given the aesthetics, particularly around the picturesque Daylesford Lake, it is not hard to see why. The added attractions here are the mineral springs, numerous walks and spa centres with a whole host of natural therapies. If you are short of time, don't miss a walk around the lake, a stroll through the centre of the town and a dip or treatment at the newly refurbished spa resort at Hepburn Springs. The visitor information centre next to the post office in Daylesford can offer all the details and provide maps (*98 Vincent St. Tel: (03) 5321 6123. www.visitdaylesford.com*). You may decide to stay for a night, in which case there are plenty of fine restaurants and accommodation. Try the **Red Star Café** in Hepburn Springs (*115 Main Rd, Hepburn Springs. Tel: (03) 5348 2297*).
From Daylesford, take the Ballan Rd to join the Western Freeway (M8) back to the Western Ring Rd and the city centre (108km/67 miles).

Tour: The Mount Macedon Ranges and Spa Country

Yarra Valley vineyards

Geographically, the Yarra Valley refers to the upper reaches of the Yarra beyond the city fringe, and it adds even more celebrity to the gracious – if not mighty – river that threads its way through the Melbourne metropolis. Here, it is not just the aesthetics or the river itself that hold great sway, but that other liquid afforded far more reverence in the form of red or white wine.

The first vines were planted in the Yarra Valley in 1838, making it the oldest wine-growing region in Australia and now, along with Barossa, Margaret River, Hunter and more recently Mornington, the valley's name has become synonymous with quality vintage.

The cool, variable climate and diverse soils produce some of the country's best Pinot Noir, Chardonnay, Cabernet Sauvignon, Merlot and Shiraz. There are over 80 cellar doors in the region producing about 19,000 metric tonnes of grapes, and grossing around AU$20 million in sales per annum. About 65 per cent of production is of reds.

Located less than an hour's drive from Melbourne, the region attracts over 2 million visitors a year, with the vineyards all trying to outdo each other with vintage quality, architecture and food. There are some fine B&Bs in the area, so overnight trips are a distinct possibility, or you might consider combining a day trip with the world-renowned Healesville Sanctuary (*see p81*).

For more information on the wineries of the Yarra, visit *www.yarravalleywine.com*. For touring, a copy of the Melbourne *Melways* map is recommended.

The following are a sample of the most popular estate cellar doors and restaurants.

View across the Tarrawarra Estate winery

Balgownle Estate

Great views from the restaurant and café, with Chardonnay and Pinot Noir as staples. Restaurant and accommodation.
Corner of Melba Hwy & Gulf Rd, Yarra Glen (Melway 267/G7).
Tel: (03) 9730 0700.
www.balgownieestate.com.au.
Open: 9am–5pm.

Fully laden vines

Domaine Chandon

Yes, that's Chandon, as in Moët and sparkling! The French have arrived and this place exudes class. Restaurant and great views.
Green Point, Maroondah Hwy, Coldstream (Melway 276/C7).
Tel: (03) 9738 9200.
www.greenpointwines.com.au.
Open: 10.30am–4.30pm.

Long Gully

A small family-owned and -run boutique vineyard offering a welcome break from the bigger and more commercial estates. Excellent Shiraz.
100 Long Gully Rd, Healesville (Melway 269/C10). Tel: (03) 9510 5798. www.longgullyestate.com.
Open: 11am–5pm.

Rochford Wines

One of the highest-profile estates with a full range of vintages. Restaurant and café.
Corner of Maroondah Hwy & Hill Rd,
Coldstream (Melway 277/D9). Tel: (03) 5962 2119. www.rochfordwines.com.
Open: 10am–5pm.

St Huberts

Established by Hubert Castella in 1862, so no shortage of history. Particularly famous for its Cabernet Sauvignon.
Corner of St Huberts Rd & Maroondah Hwy, Coldstream (Melway 275/K12). Tel: (03) 9739 1118. www.sthuberts.com.au. Open: Mon–Fri 9.30am–5pm, Sat & Sun 10.30am–5.30pm.

Yering Station

Set on the site of the valley's first 1838 vineyard. Restaurant, gardens, children's playground and art gallery.
38 Melba Hwy, Yarra Glen (Melway 275/C6). Tel: (03) 9730 0100. www.yering.com. Open: Mon–Fri 10am–5pm, Sat & Sun 10am–6pm.

Drive: Yarra Ranges National Park and Healesville

Forming part of the southern fringe of the Great Dividing Range and source of the state's best-known river, the 76,000ha (187,800-acre) Yarra Ranges National Park is one of the most beautiful in Victoria. This scenic drive also explores the rural town of Healesville, home to a world-class native wildlife sanctuary. See page 61 for map.

Allow a whole day. Total distance 241km (150 miles).

From the centre of Melbourne, head northeast via SH34 (Whitehorse Rd/Maroondah Hwy) to Lilydale. Just beyond Lilydale, turn right onto the B380 (Warburton Hwy) to Warburton (36km/22 miles). At Warburton, follow signs to Mount Donna Buang (right, Mount Donna Buang Rd). Continue to the Rainforest Gallery (8km/5 miles).

1 Mount Donna Buang and the Rainforest Gallery

The Rainforest Gallery, with its 40m (131ft) observation deck and boardwalk, provides a fine introduction to the lush forest of the Yarra Ranges. From the Rainforest Gallery, head up to the 1,245m (4085ft) summit of Mount Donna Buang (8km/ 5 miles), where the expansive views are enhanced by a 21m (69ft) lookout tower.

Return to Warburton and continue northeast along the C511 to Reefton (29km/18 miles). At Reefton, follow signs (right) to Upper Yarra Dam.

2 Upper Yarra Dam

The reservoir encompasses pleasant open parklands and some fine views from the 90m (295ft) dam wall, which can be reached by car. The Upper Yarra is the third largest of the city's nine main supply dams. Of historical interest in the park grounds is the restored McVeigh's

Taggerty River, Yarra Ranges National Park

Water Wheel, which used to power the old hotel (now underwater).

Back on the C511, drive up and through the forest to the junction with the C513 (21km/13 miles). Turn left and drive 9km (6 miles) to the turn-off to Lake Mountain Resort (signposted). Climb to the resort car park.

3 Lake Mountain Resort

From mid-June to early October (provided there is snow cover) Lake Mountain (1,480m/4,855ft) serves as a major regional cross-country skiing resort. At other times this same network provides excellent walking, with the mountain summit (*500m/550yds from the car park*) attracting people year-round for its viewpoints. The basic resort facilities remain operational off-season, including the restaurant and café.
Tel: (03) 5957 7222.
www.lakemountainresort.com.au.
Free admission in summer, admission charge in winter season.
Return to the C513 and continue northwest to Marysville (21km/13 miles).

4 Marysville

The once beautiful sub-Alpine village of Marysville was effectively razed during the 'Black Saturday' bush fires of February 2009, with the loss of 47 lives and almost all of its built structures. Although the bush is regenerating, little remains of the village itself and until it is reconstructed it is a sad testament to the devastation that bush fires can

cause. Local natural sights still worth seeing include the 84m (275ft) Steavenson Falls (*4km/2 miles from Marysville*).
From Marysville, head southwest via the C512 and through the towering mountain ash alongside the B360 to Healesville (37km/23 miles).

5 Healesville

Healesville is the main service town in the Yarra Valley, and is home to one of the country's oldest and best wildlife sanctuaries. The **Healesville Sanctuary** was founded in 1934 and has over 200 native species. Of particular note is the 'Platypusary', which, as the name suggests, is where the notoriously bizarre creatures can be viewed underwater.
Badger Creek Rd, Healesville (4km/2½ miles south of the town centre). Tel: (03) 5957 2800. www.zoo.org.au. Open: 9am–5pm. Admission charge. From Healesville, head west on the B360 (Maroondah Hwy) to Lilydale (22km/14 miles) and back to the city.

Lake Mountain ski resort in 'full slide'

The Great Ocean Road to Adelaide

Completed quite literally with buckets and spades between 1918 and 1932, the Great Ocean Road is Australia's premier scenic coastal drive, home to one of its most recognisable icons, the Twelve Apostles. Monolithic and defiant in their losing battle to the Southern Ocean, they feature in glossy magazines, alongside Uluru and the Opera House, as the quintessential 'come see Australia' icon.

When it was first conceived in the early 1900s, some bright spark (in this case the then mayor of Geelong, Howard Hitchcock) decided to call his planned coastal route to Warrnambool the 'Great Ocean Road'. Had he not done so, it may have naturally assumed its other name, the B100 – hardly conducive to packing your own bucket and spade and hitting the road! The Great Ocean Road it became, and the tourism marketeers are now delirious because 'great' is only the half of it!

Geelong acts as gatekeeper to the mighty B100 and tries hard to delay you with its impressive waterfront and colourful 'bollard people'. Further attempts are made by the congenial and beach-clad Bellarine Peninsula before the Surf Coast succeeds with 'Winki Pop's' sandy bottom – provided you can stay upright, of course.

So, already coastally primed, your journey – and the road proper – starts in Torquay, where the 'oohs' and 'aahs' sound with increasing repetition as the beautiful scenery unfolds. First is Lorne, one of the most popular of the coast's many holiday resort towns and villages, followed by Apollo Bay, which is backed by the lush rainforest and waterfalls of the Otway National Park. Time for a lighthouse? No problem. Cape Otway's happens to be the country's oldest and

THE GREAT OCEAN ROAD DRIVING DISTANCES AND TIMES

Melbourne to Geelong	72km (45 miles)	1 hour
Geelong to Torquay	37km (23 miles)	35 mins
Torquay to Lorne	45km (28 miles)	1 hour
Lorne to Apollo Bay	45km (28 miles)	1 hour
Apollo Bay to Port Campbell	96km (60 miles)	3 hours
Port Campbell to Warrnambool	66km (41 miles)	2½ hours
Warrnambool to Adelaide	663km (412 miles)	8 hours

you can even stay there overnight. From the Otways, the 'ol' B' turns inland temporarily before hitting the coast again at Princetown and the Port Campbell National Park. There you can muse upon those Apostles and numerous other dramatic, appealing, yet doomed, rock formations. From the last of its major stacks – London Bridge – it is inland again until Warrnambool, the coast's biggest town, and Port Fairy, its prettiest. Between mid-July and mid-September this is a great place to see calving southern right whales.

Once across the state border, it's a steady drive to Adelaide, the most English of Australian cities. With its infectiously laid-back atmosphere and gracious aesthetics, it is hard to pull yourself away to the wealth of natural scenic delights on offer in the Fleurieu Peninsula or Kangaroo Island. Then, looming large physically are the Adelaide Hills, where cool takes on both meanings amid lofty viewpoints, heritage villages and vineyards. Time for the Barossa, a little wine tasting and a spectacular dent in the budget. Finally, with that northern horizon beckoning, you get the chance to see the outback at Flinders and Wilpena.

GEELONG AND THE BELLARINE PENINSULA
Geelong
With a population of just over 200,000, Geelong is the second-largest city in Victoria. Its people are a relaxed, predominantly working-class bunch,

The Great Ocean Road to Adelaide (1)

The Great Ocean Road near Lorne

had diversified to become the manufacturing hub of the state. Recent years have seen a decline, particularly in car manufacturer Ford Australia.

For the tourist or casual visitor, Geelong is gatekeeper to the Bellarine Peninsula, the Surf Coast and the world-renowned Great Ocean Road. Yet with so many oceanic delights beckoning from beyond, it is perhaps not surprising that the city struggles to attract visitors for very long. This challenge has been met quite admirably by the city fathers, particularly with the development of the showpiece **Waterfront**, **Eastern Beach** and **Eastern Park** (and **Botanic Gardens**), and a day on the beach or a picnic there will soon apply the mental brakes to those oceanic aspirations. The best place to park is on the fringes of Eastern Park. The Waterfront has all the features you might expect, from cafés and ocean swimming pools to the carousel. Another major attraction in the town is the **National Wool Museum** (*26 Moorabool St. Tel: (03) 5272 4701. www.geelongaustralia.com.au. Open: Mon–Fri 9.30am–5pm, Sat & Sun 1–5pm. Admission charge*).

Just before you arrive in Geelong you will find the Geelong and Great Ocean Road **Visitor Information Centre** (*Cnr Princes Hwy and St George's Rd, Corio. Tel: 1800 620 888. www. greatoceanroad.org. Open: 9am–5pm*).

Bellarine Peninsula

South and east of Geelong is the Bellarine Peninsula which, like the

proud of their independence (despite the diminishing green belt that separates them from Melbourne) and even more so of their great Australian Rules Football team 'The Cats'. A port city 74km (46 miles) from Melbourne, Geelong was first settled three weeks after Melbourne in 1838. Like that of all the early settlements, its early development was manifest in agriculture, particularly the wool industry. By the mid-1900s, the city

Mornington Peninsula, has been a holiday spot in demand with Melbournians for many years. Although not yet blessed (or cursed) with the same 'How much?' real-estate prices or sheer number and variety of beaches as its close neighbour, it remains a deservingly popular place to visit. Here the beaches and views on offer in Queenscliff (32km/20 miles from Geelong), Ocean Grove and Barwon Heads will certainly not disappoint. Queenscliff, which has a connecting vehicular ferry to Sorrento, is the most visited destination and is noted for its 19th-century buildings, pier and military fort.

GEELONG'S BOLLARD PEOPLE

Perhaps the most attractive features of Geelong's multi-million-dollar showpiece Waterfront are the enchanting and colourful 'Bollard People'. Created by local artist Jan Mitchell, there are more than 100 of the life-size figures dotted along the beachfront, depicting prominent characters from the city's history. They include surf lifesavers, sailors, beach belles and football players. Beginning in 1994, it took Mitchell and her team four years to create the bollards from old timber piles recovered from the city's demolished Yarra Street pier.

Queenscliff Visitor Information Centre. 55 Hesse St. Tel: 1300 884 843. www.queenscliff.org. Open: 9am–5pm.

The Great Ocean Road to Adelaide

Two 'Bollard People' along Geelong's waterfront

'Winki Pop', 'The Barrel' and the Rip Curl Pro!

For those from colder climes, who grew up in the knowledge that in winter a 'wee dip in the ocean' could result in death by hypothermia inside three minutes, the very concept of surfing may be a complete enigma. It looks a lot of fun, but given that most non-Antipodeans cannot stay upright on a shopping mall escalator, let alone a surfboard, why would you try it? And besides, what about those sharks?

For Australians, who have been able to stay upright on a surfboard almost from foetal stage, or at least before being able to build a sand-castle, surfing is as automatic and as much a part of life as cleaning one's teeth. Surfies look at the sunburn brigade from the northern hemisphere sheltering under a handkerchief or dipping their toes in the wavelets and just shake their blond tousled locks. And the sharks? On that matter it's 'Yeah, seen a few, no worries mate.'

So, to the uninitiated, Bells Beach looks like any other ocean beach and a place of reverent beauty in its own right. The doorstep to sharks and fish, perhaps? Well, no, apparently it's an awful lot more than that. To those board owners who have mastered the great art, this little bay is of almost spiritual significance, and when the surf is up at Bells (and the luscious-sounding 'Winki Pop' surf break) it is quite simply world class. Equally good is 'The Barrel'.

It all began over 60 years ago when a few locals lugged their 5m- (16ft-)

Bells Beach is a favourite among surfers

Two surfers check out the waves before trying out their skills

long boards to the isolated beach to ride the waves. In those days, due to board design and materials it was a relatively small-scale sport, but by the late 1950s the first competition was held at Bells (with prize money of $2) and its future was written in the sand.

By the mid-1960s, the event, then called the Bells Beach Easter Rally, had grown and was attracting surfers from around Australia. By the early 1970s, board design was developing and the boards were becoming smaller, faster and lighter. Along with the big brand-name sponsorship, the sport and the event had become fully professional and certainly worth a lot more than $2. Now the Rip Curl Pro Surfing Festival is held every Easter and has become an event of global standing.

Visitors are welcome at Bells and the venue is classed as 'intermediate'. For non-surfers, it is a great place to watch how it ought to be done – but like skiing or golf it is much harder than it looks. For the initiated, the official statistics are (by all accounts):

Best tide: All tides
Best swell direction: SW
Best size: 0.6–6m (2–20ft)
Best wind: NW, N, W
Bottom: Sand
Bring: Shortboard, mid-range and gun
Best season: Year-round
Access and parking: Easy and good
Shark danger: 2
Frankly, this doesn't make any novice feel any more informed, bar the sandy bottom. You'll get that, literally.

TORQUAY TO PETERBOROUGH
The Surf Coast

First stop for serious surfies or 'Apostle' hunters along the Great Ocean Road is Torquay, capital of the Surf Coast. It has a number of fine recreational and surf beaches, with one reaching almost legendary status. **Bells Beach** is home to 'Winki Pop', 'The Barrel' and the Rip Curl Pro! It is about 10km (6 miles) west of Torquay and spectators are welcome. Torquay also has some fine beaches and it is worth popping in to the **Surf World Museum**, said to be the world's largest surfing museum (*Beach Rd. Tel: (03) 5261 4606. www.surfworld.org.au. Open: 9am–5pm. Admission charge*).

Lorne

Backed by the **Great Otway National Park** and nestled near Point Grey, Lorne makes the most of its combination of bush and beach. With its lauded café culture and range of stylish accommodation, it provides an ideal stop. You may also be lured by the walk to **Erskine Falls** (9km/6 miles signposted off Mountjoy Parade). *Torquay Visitor Information Centre. 15 Mountjoy Parade. Tel: (03) 5289 1152. www.visitsurfcoast.com*

Apollo Bay and Cape Otway

From Lorne, the Great Ocean Road winds its way past headlands and through small river valleys to Apollo Bay. The area is home to many artists and musicians, adding colour and character. Try to coincide your visit with the weekly market held on the Foreshore (*Sat 8.30am–4.30pm*). Fishing is hugely popular from Apollo Bay, both commercial and recreational.

Not to be missed is the short walk (30 mins) from Maits Rest (*17km/ 11 miles west of the town*) typifying the lush rainforest of the **Great Otway National Park**, and also **Cape Otway** with its famous 1848 **lighthouse** – the oldest in Australia (*turn off 20km/12 miles west*). It has a café and keeper's cottage accommodation (*Tel: (03) 5237 9240. www.lightstation.com. Open: 9am–5pm. Admission charge for tours*).

The Twelve Apostles

At Princetown, 50km (31 miles) west of Cape Otway, after a spell inland road meets ocean again at the **Port Campbell National Park**. This limestone plateau has been battered and sculpted by the southern ocean, almost reluctantly giving in with 'last stand' formations of towers, caves and arches. There are names like Pudding Basin, Razorback and the Grotto, but most famous are the Twelve Apostles. Forget counting the stacks, there are not twelve now, but eight. In an ongoing process, number nine was lost to the waves in 2005. The **Twelve Apostles Interpretative Centre** has all the details (*Tel: 131 963*).

Loch Ard Gorge

At Loch Ard Gorge there is an excellent clifftop walk with a staircase leading to

Loch Ard Gorge offers a scenic walk with a staircase leading to the beach

the beach. It was here that the Scottish immigrant ship *Loch Ard* came to grief in 1878, losing 52 lives.

From Loch Ard, the lookouts over the Arch and London Bridge rock formations beckon before the Great Ocean Road turns inland at Peterborough towards Warrnambool.

WARRNAMBOOL TO THE MURRAY RIVER
Warrnambool

One of the oldest towns in the state, Warrnambool was first settled permanently from about 1839 and was a busy port throughout the 19th century. Ironically, it was sealers and whalers who were first attracted to the sheltered waters of Lady Bay, which is now the venue for the town's biggest tourist attraction – whale-watching. Between mid-July and mid-September, southern right whales (that were hunted to near extinction) come to the bay to calve and are visible close to the shore about 80 per cent of the time. There are free viewing platforms at **Logans Beach** (*East via Logans Beach Rd and off Hopkins Point Rd*). For the latest sighting reports, *tel: 1800 637 725.*

The **Flagstaff Hill Maritime Museum** provides a fascinating insight into the region's eventful maritime past, to which almost 200 shipwrecks attest. The sorry inventory includes the immigrant ship *Loch Ard* (*89 Merri St. Tel: (03) 5559 4600. www.flagstaffhill.com. Open: 9am–5pm. Admission charge*).

Port Fairy

This fishing village, nestled beside the Moyne River, is arguably the most attractive of all the settlements along the Great Ocean Road. It owes its

The picturesque wharf at Port Fairy

existence to sealers and whalers who settled here in the 1820s and 1830s. *Port Fairy Visitor Information Centre. Railway Pl. Tel: (03) 5568 2682. www.portfairy.com.au*

Portland and around

Portland is Victoria's earliest permanent European settlement, founded in 1834 by the Henry brothers. Though lacking the charm and atmosphere of Port Fairy, there are a number of interesting attractions including the **vintage cable tram** that trundles along a 7km (4-mile) track taking in various sights like the **Botanic Gardens** (*Tel: (03) 5523 2831. www.portlandcabletrams.com.au. Open: daily. Admission charge*).

The stunning scenery of **Cape Nelson** and **Cape Bridgewater**, southwest of the town, offers the highest coastal cliffs in the state, dramatic rock features, isolated beaches, and a large fur seal colony.

From Portland you can either head inland along the A1 (*Princes Hwy*) to Mount Gambier (*114km/71 miles away*) or continue along the coast to Nelson, where you can visit the **Princess Margaret Rose Cave** with its impressive display of stalagmites and stalactites (*Tel: (08) 8738 4171. www.princessmargaretrosecave.com. Open: 10.30am–4.30pm. Admission charge*).

Mount Gambier to the Murray River

Just west of the Victoria–South Australia border, the commercial nature of Mount Gambier makes its caves and volcanic crater lakes an unlikely tourist attraction. As well as a few minor caves in the city, the main attraction is **Blue Lake**, a deep pool in the centre of an extinct volcanic crater that changes colour from grey-green in winter to turquoise-blue in summer.

From Mount Gambier, the Princes Highway heads north to Kingston before skirting the lengthy **Younghusband Peninsula** to the mouth of the mighty Murray River. The **Coorong National Park** takes up a large part of the peninsula, and if you have a 4WD it is worth investigating the quiet campsites and lagoons, which are rich in wildlife.

Fleurieu Peninsula

Named by Captain Nicolas Baudin in 1802 after the French Navy Minister, this peninsula south of Adelaide

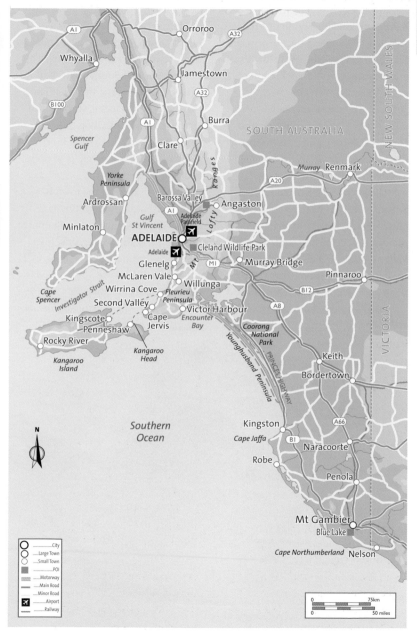

Orroroo

A32

A1

Whyalla

Jamestown

A32

B100

Burra

Spencer
Gulf

SOUTH AUSTRALIA

A1

Clare

NEW SOUTH WALES

Murray Renmark

A20

Yorke
Peninsula

Lofty Ranges

Barossa Valley

A1

Angaston

Ardrossan

Adelaide
Parafield

Minlaton

Gulf
St Vincent

ADELAIDE

Adelaide

Cleland Wildlife Park

Glenelg

M1

Murray Bridge

McLaren Vale

Pinnaroo

Cape
Spencer

Investigator Strait

Wirrina Cove

Willunga

B12

Second Valley

Fleurieu
Peninsula

Victor Harbour

A8

Kingscote

Cape
Jervis

Encounter
Bay

Penneshaw

Coorong
National
Park

VICTORIA

Rocky River

Kangaroo
Head

Keith

Kangaroo
Island

Younghusband Peninsula

PRINCES HIGHWAY

Bordertown

N

Southern
Ocean

Kingston

A66

Cape Jaffa

B1

Naracoorte

Robe

Penola

Mt Gambier

Blue Lake

Cape Northumberland Nelson

City
Large Town
Small Town
POI
Motorway
Main Road
Minor Road
Airport
Railway

0		75km
0		50 miles

possesses a diverse range of landscapes and towns. Central to its tourist appeal is the wine-growing region of **McLaren Vale** and **Willunga** in the northwest. Marketed as the place where 'the vines meet the sea', grapes were first planted in 1838 and there are now over 60 vineyards in the region, many with cellar doors. The **McLaren Vale and Fleurieu Visitor Centre** can supply all the details (*Main Rd. Tel: (08) 8323 9944. www.mclarenvale.info*).

McLaren Vale is bordered to the west by some excellent **beaches** including Maslin Beach, Port Willunga and Aldinga Beach. Further west, **Second Valley** is a fine precursor to the rugged coastline of **Cape Jervis**, departure point for the ferry to Kangaroo Island.

Tucked into the southeastern corner and sheltered by Encounter Bay is **Victor Harbour**, the peninsula's largest town. Founded by European whalers in the 1830s, it is now a holiday town for Adelaidians, and a fine venue for whale-watching. The newly renovated **South Australian Whale Centre** tells of the leviathan's tragic, yet now hopeful, story. It also organises whale-watching tours (*Railway Terrace. Tel: (08) 8551 0750. www.sawhalecentre.com. Open: daily. Admission charge*).

Another feature of the town is **Granite Island**, linked to the shore by a 600m (1,970ft) long jetty and home to around 2,000 **Fairy Penguins**. Many 'happy feet' come ashore at dusk to roost in their burrows, and guided watching tours are available (*Tel: (08) 8552 7555. www.graniteisland.com.au. Admission charge*).

One of the Remarkable Rocks on Kangaroo Island

Granite Island is home to 2,000 Fairy Penguins

The **Victor Harbour Visitor Information Centre** is on the Esplanade (*The Causeway Building, The Esplanade. Tel: (08) 8551 0777. www.victor.sa.gov.au*).

Kangaroo Island

At 4,405sq km (1,701sq miles), Kangaroo Island is Australia's third-largest island, and a tour of at least three days is recommended.

The island has an impressive native wildlife list and many other wonderful natural attractions, from the intriguing **Remarkable Rocks** formation, coastal caves, cliffs and arches, to farmed honeybees all encompassed within the protective realm of 19 national and conservation parks.

The main centres of population on the island are at **Kingscote** and **Penneshaw** (both ferry ports) situated in the northeast corner.

The island was named Kangaroo in 1802 by British explorer Matthew Flinders, not because he encountered those now iconic 'sheep on springs', but because he landed at Kangaroo Head. Indeed, if the island were to earn such a wildlife-oriented name, it should perhaps be Koala Island, as it is home to a veritable plague of these animals. In fact, in recent years a programme of surgical sterilisation has had to take place. Regardless, this is your big chance to see koala in the wild.

The Kangaroo Island Gateway Visitor Information Centre. Howard Drive, Penneshaw. Tel: (08) 8553 1185. www.tourkangarooisland.com.au

Adelaide

Founded in 1836 and wedged between the Mount Lofty Ranges and Gulf St Vincent, Adelaide is a gracious city with a population of 1 million. Known for its heritage buildings, broad streets and

GETTING TO KANGAROO ISLAND

Sealink ferries (vehicle/passenger) make the crossing from Cape Jervis to Penneshaw four times a day. The 13km (8-mile) crossing takes 45 minutes.
Tel: 131 301. www.sealink.com.au. Fares vary.

The North Terrace, Adelaide

spacious parks, it has a distinctly European feel that extends beyond aesthetics to lifestyle, with a thriving café culture and as many restaurants per capita as Sydney or Melbourne. With the Barossa Valley (Australia's best-known wine region), the Adelaide Hills, Fleurieu Peninsula and Kangaroo Island all within easy reach, you'll find a lack of time your only problem.
South Australian Visitor and Travel Centre. 18 King William St. Tel: 1300 655 276. www.southaustralia.com. Open: Mon–Fri 8.30am–5pm, Sat & Sun 9am–2pm. Adelaide Airport branch open: 6am–late.
For information on public transport: Passenger Transport Infoline. Tel: 1300 311 108. www.adelaidemetro.com.au

Adelaide Zoo

Just a short walk from the city centre, this is one of the country's best zoos, with a strong conservation ethic. There is a fine collection of the traditional and native fauna, and you will be struck by how lush the zoo is. The biggest attractions at Adelaide Zoo are Wang Wang and Funi, two giant pandas given to Australia by the Chinese government in December 2009.
Frome Rd. Tel: (08) 8267 3255. www.zoossa.com.au. Open: 9.30am–5pm. Admission charge.

Botanic Gardens

With a classic English-style ambience, the Botanic Gardens offer a tranquil retreat from the city. There is a grand conservatory built for the Bicentennial and a 19th-century Palm House.
North Terrace. Tel: (08) 8222 9311. www.environment.sa.gov.au. Open: Mon–Fri 7.30am–6.30pm, Sat & Sun 9am–6.30pm.

Central Market

Over 135 years old, Adelaide's Central Market has more than 80 multifarious, multi-cultural food stalls selling everything from peppers to poppadoms.

The Adelaide Botanic Gardens

The intriguing architecture adds another dimension to the National Wine Centre of Australia, Adelaide

Grote & Gouger Sts (off Victoria Sq).
Tel: (04) 0216 5800.
www.centralmarkettour.com.au. Open:
Tue 7am–5.30pm, Thur 9am–5.30pm,
Fri 7am–9pm, Sat 7am–3pm. Admission
charge for tours.

Glenelg
On the shores of Gulf St Vincent and
about 10km (6 miles) from Adelaide,
Glenelg is the city's favourite beachside
suburb and the site where Captain John
Hindmarsh, the first governor, landed
in 1836. Cafés and restaurants abound
– all close to the calm, shallow waters of
the gulf. The **City to Bay tram** is a good
way to get there (*Tel: (08) 8218 2362.*
www.adelaidemetro.com.au).

National Wine Centre of Australia
Given the popularity and quality of
South Australian wines, it would be
rude not to present them in a manner
befitting a vintage in the heart of the
state capital. The striking modern
façade houses a cellar of 32,000
Australian wines, a tasting gallery, shop
and information about where to visit
the region's best cellar doors.
Corner of Botanic & Hackney Rds
(southeast corner of Botanic Gardens).
Tel: (08) 8303 3355.
www.wineaustralia.com.au. Open:
Mon–Fri 9am–5pm, Sat & Sun
10am–5pm. Free admission (charge for
tastings). Bus: City Loop 99C.

South Australian Museum
Commanding a prime spot on North
Terrace, this museum's flagship display
is the fascinating Australian Aboriginal
Cultures Gallery, containing the world's
largest collection of Aboriginal
artefacts, records and photographs.

There is also an in-depth look at the life of Antarctic explorer Sir Douglas Mawson, and impressive displays covering anthropology, natural history and science.

North Terrace. Tel: (08) 8207 7500. www.samuseum.sa.gov.au. Open: 10am–5pm. Free admission.

Adelaide Hills

Think of South Australia and the word 'desert' springs to mind, with 'hot' coming right behind it. It's not surprising that the elevations and subsequent cooling influence of the Mount Lofty Ranges are very welcome, possessing those lovely assets called seasons and, when it comes to visitation, the equivalent of Adelaide's 'fridge'.

The hills, with that classic rolling landscape and country feel, are only 10km (6 miles) from the city of Adelaide and have been spared development by a string of national and conservation parks. Noted for their pretty countryside, vineyards and historic villages, at times it is easy to forget you are in Australia. A fine place to start your exploration is **Mount Lofty** (727m/2,385ft) which, provided the weather is fine, affords a superb view over the city and beyond (*Mount Lofty Summit Rd. Tel: (08) 8339 2600. www.mtloftysummit.com*).

Nearby, the **Cleland Wildlife Park** (*Summit Rd. Tel: (08) 8339 2444. www.parks.sa.gov.au. Open: 9.30am–5pm. Admission charge*) has a fine collection of native wildlife with mobs of free-roaming kangaroos and bilbies (small marsupials).

Other areas not to be missed are the gorge and vineyards of the **Torrens Valley** and the village of **Hahndorf** in the Onkaparinga Valley. German immigrants first settled Hahndorf in 1839 and their influence prevails.

The Barossa Valley, seen from the Mount Lofty Ranges

KANGAROO STATISTICS

There are over 60 species of kangaroo in Australia, with the Eastern Grey the most commonly seen along the east coast. All roos (except the tree kangaroo) are perfectly adapted for speed. They have evolved to conserve a remarkable amount of energy in motion, with their thick tails acting as a counterbalance. A red kangaroo (an outback species and the biggest) can reach up to 65km (40 miles) an hour and can jump further than 12m (40ft). Clearing a 3m (10ft) fence at speed would not be an issue.

The Barossa Valley

Along with Hunter, Yarra and Margaret River the words Barossa Valley are synonymous with fine wine. Only about 60km (40 miles) north of Adelaide, Australia's oldest wine-growing region is based on over 150 years of German settlement. There are around 50 cellar door wineries, with the usual impressive heritage and modern façades, quality restaurants and stylish accommodation.

The main towns of **Nuriootpa** and **Tanunda** lie along the backbone of the valley, while picturesque **Angaston**, originally established by wealthy English free settlers in the 1830s, sits in a valley of its own.

At least two days' touring is recommended, along with a firm promise to yourself to either stick to budget or blow it – spectacularly! If you do not have an agenda, try to mix the old with the new, the large with the small, the best view, best café and so on. Alternatively, take one of the many well-established, organised tours.

Food, music and art also play an important role. Beyond the restaurants there is a **Farmers' Market** in Angaston (*Sat 7.30–11.30am*) and you may catch one of the region's many convivial events and festivals, like the Barossa Vintage Festival held in April. A good place to plan your trip is at the National Wine Centre of Australia in Adelaide, but the Barossa **Visitor Information Centre** will help ensure your tour is a memorable one (*66–68 Murray St, Tanunda. Tel: (08) 8563 0600. www.barossa.com*).

The Barossa Valley is famous for its wines

Tour: Clare Valley to the Flinders Ranges

With only 1.6 people per sq km (4.2 per sq mile), South Australia typifies the term 'outback'. It is one thing to experience the urban attractions of Adelaide, or the Barossa Valley dressed in its lush ribbons of vines, but another thing altogether to venture beyond that northern horizon.

This tour takes you to the state's best-known outback attraction, the crater-like Wilpena Pound and the Flinders Ranges National Park, once described by Australian artist Sir Hans Heysen as a place where 'the bones of nature are laid bare'.

Allow at least 5 days. Total distance: 850km (528 miles).

From Adelaide, head north on the Barrier Hwy (A32) past Gawler to Giles Corner (87km/54 miles). At Giles Corner, follow the B82 to Clare (50km/31 miles).

1 Clare Valley

Jesuit priests were the first to plant vines in the Clare Valley in 1851, and ever since it has produced some of Australia's best wines, particularly Rieslings. The valley has over 30 wineries, many with cellar doors. One of the most popular is **Sevenhill Cellars**, the oldest (*College Rd. Sevenhill. Tel: (08) 8843 4222. www.sevenhillcellars.com.au. Open:*

Mon–Fri 9am–5pm, Sat & Sun 10am–5pm).

There is a good range of accommodation on offer in the area and the **Clare Visitor Information Centre** can assist with bookings (*Corner of Main North & Spring Gully Rds. Tel: 1800 242 131. www.clarevalley.com.au. Open: Mon–Fri 9am–5pm, Sat 9.30am–4.30pm, Sun 10am–4pm). From Clare, head east back to the Barrier Hwy (A32) and north to Burra (43km/27 miles).*

2 Burra

Amid the barren landscape around the aptly named **Bald Hills Range** is the former copper mining town of Burra. Established in 1851, at its height the town's mines produced 5 per cent of the world supply, but within 20 years the supply was exhausted. There are many relics that are best explored on the self-guided Heritage Trail. Details are available from the visitor centre

(Market Sq. Tel: (08) 8892 2154.
www.visitburra.com. Open: 9am–5pm).
From Burra, continue north on
the Barrier Hwy (A32) to Terowie
(63km/39 miles). At Terowie, take the
B56 to Orroroo, then the B80 to Hawker
(166km/103 miles). At Hawker, follow
signs to the Flinders Ranges National
Park and Wilpena (51km/32 miles).

3 Flinders Ranges National Park

The Flinders Ranges National Park
(912sq km/352sq miles) represents
only a fraction of the Flinders Ranges
themselves, but contains some of
their most striking and beautiful
geological features.

The most spectacular is **Wilpena
Pound**, not a vast crater left from an
asteroid, but in fact an extraordinary
natural amphitheatre ringed by sheer
cliffs and buttresses. Almost defying
logic, the ridge assumes an appealing
palette of colours under the oceanic
skies. There are various locations
from which to view the pound and
you can explore the area either by foot,
road or air. Your likely accommodation
establishment, the Wilpena Pound
Resort, can advise *(Wilpena Rd.*
Tel: (08) 8648 0004.
www.wilpenapound.com.au).
From Wilpena, return to Hawker
then continue on the B83 to Port
Augusta (160km/99 miles). After an
overnight stay in Port Augusta, you
can head south on the Princes Hwy
(A1) back to Adelaide (400km/
249 miles).

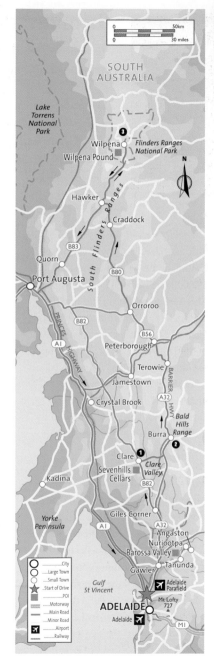

Tasmania

Tasmania is Australia's second-smallest, most southerly and only island state. It is about the same size as Ireland, or West Virginia in the USA. It suffers from 'Little Island Syndrome' which, when you sit alongside the largest island on earth, is understandable. As a result, Little Tassie gets left off maps and holiday agendas, and it is almost mocked or bullied by the mainland. However, like most things small, mocked and bullied, the island actually has incredible depth and beauty.

Originally part of the mainland as little as 10,000 years ago, Tasmania was inhabited by Aboriginals for over 35,000 years before Dutch navigator Abel Tasman put it on the world map in 1642. Tasman named it Van Diemen's Land after the governor of the Dutch East Indies Company, but was unaware that it was an island. After James Cook's voyage of discovery added more detail in 1777, Tasmania was formally inhabited by the British from Sydney in 1803 in order to prevent the French from claiming it. As a result, Hobart is the second-oldest capital in Australia. Famously, from 1833 until the 1850s, Van Diemen's Land was a destination for the hardest of convicted British and Irish criminals, and Port Arthur was considered nothing short of hell on earth. Yet with the closure of the infamous jail in 1877 (together with a name change to Tasmania in 1856 to try to shake off the negative notoriety), free settlement began in earnest. Due to a combination of climate, geography and geology, immigration has never reached the same extent as the mainland, hence the state remains undeveloped and unspoilt.

Forget the iconic Australian images when in Tasmania. There are no endless red deserts, vast distances to travel, no Gold Coasts or commercial theme parks. Here it is parks of an altogether different nature and, unlike the rest of the country, the scale seems as much vertical as horizontal. Over a third of the state is protected as a World Heritage National Park. Large parts of it are as remote and inaccessible as they are beautiful. This is 'tiger country', literally: a place where some believe the Tasmanian Tiger (Thylacine), a species that was declared extinct in the 1930s, might still exist.

Stunning coastal and mountain scenery predominates, but the state's human story and the modern struggle to conserve that inherent beauty are both fascinating and admirable. Tasmanians are a friendly bunch who ignore the mainland's negative perceptions, get on with life and are more than delighted to introduce you to their incredible backyard.

At least ten days is recommended to tour the island's major sights, preferably more given the more southerly, changeable weather.

You can fly cheaply from Melbourne and Sydney to Hobart and Launceston, or bring your own vehicle on the *Spirit* (overnight ferry) from Melbourne. Once there, you will find travelling around straightforward and driving distances manageable. One thing is for sure; you won't be in a hurry to get back.

For information about Tasmania, visit www.discovertasmania.com

Tasmania

Tasmania

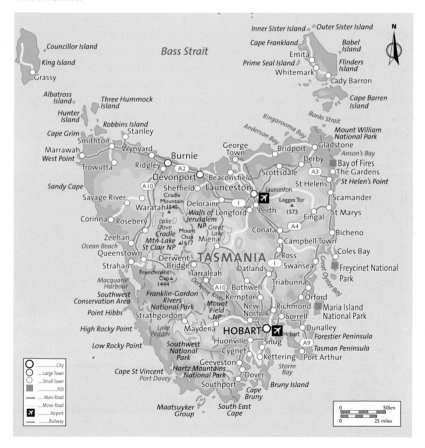

THE TASMANIAN FERRY

The *Spirit of Tasmania* ferry (*Spirit* for short) operates between Melbourne and Devonport, sailing from both locations most nights and some days during peak periods (*see www.spiritoftasmania.com.au*). The journey takes 11 hours. The basic cost of a standard vehicle varies depending on length and type of vehicle; passenger fare is not inclusive. Passengers have the option of de-luxe en-suite cabins, basic cabins or the famed Ocean Seat Recliners. The latter are similar to business class on commercial airliners; however, you will not be alone but in close proximity to a large number of others.

Hobart

With a population of just over 200,000, Hobart is Tasmania's largest city and the state's capital. Settled in 1803 in a strategic maritime position on the Derwent River estuary, initially it was a penal colony before steadily morphing into the administrative and financial heart of the state. It is one of Australia's oldest settlements, reflected by the many heritage buildings that surround its iconic waterfront. It was named after Lord Hobart, the then Colonial Secretary. Fringing the western suburbs is the 1,271m (4,170ft) Mount Wellington, the city's most dominant natural feature.

The waterfront and original docks form the historic heart of the city and offer the best in character and aesthetics. Sitting side by side, **Victoria Dock** and **Constitution Dock** are home to colourful fleets of fishing boats that supply the region's many seafood restaurants. To the south, behind **Princes Wharf**, is **Salamanca Place** and **Battery Point**, the site where European settlement began. Although Europeans may find the old Georgian buildings and cottages fairly unremarkable

The bustling Salamanca Market in Hobart is considered one of the best in Australia

compared to those back home, it is worth remembering that the oldest are still relative infants, being just 200 years of age. Despite that, they retain their character, and along Salamanca Place the modern attractions of arts and craft galleries, restaurants and pubs meld well together. Sadly, the same cannot be said for the modern **Salamanca Square** behind it. In stark contrast this is an example of how modern Australian architecture can ruin the historical bedrock. Salamanca Place is the venue for one of the great tourist attractions of the state – the **Salamanca Market**, held every Saturday. It is a colourful and eclectic affair worth experiencing.

At the western (inland) end of Salamanca Place, take a stroll through **St David's Park**. This was the original burial ground for Hobart, and many fascinating headstones remain. To the right of the park is **Parliament House**, built by convict labour around 1840.

Nearby, the **Tasmanian Museum and Art Gallery** has a small but impressive collection showcasing the island's natural and social history. The story surrounding the fate of the island's Aboriginals is particularly moving (*40 Macquarie St. Tel: (03) 6211 4177. www.tmag.tas.gov.au. Open: 10am–5pm. Free admission*).

The city's strong maritime links are well represented in the **Hobart Maritime Museum** (*Carnegie Building, corner of Davey and Argyle Sts. Tel: (03) 6234 1427. www.maritimetas.org. Open: 9am–5pm. Free admission for children*).

Cascade Brewery is Australia's oldest

If your visit coincides with fine weather, a drive (22km/14 miles) to the summit of **Mount Wellington** is highly recommended, especially at dawn (*West of the city, follow signs off the B64*). On a clear day, you will be treated to expansive views of the city below and to the headlands of the Tasman Peninsula, Maria and Bruny islands, even the peaks of Mount Freycinet 100km (62 miles) away. However, it can be both windy and cold.

On the way back down the mountain, it is worth calling in at the historic **Cascade Brewery**, Australia's oldest (*131 Cascade Rd. Tel: (03) 6224 1117. www.cascadebrewery.com.au. Open: daily. Charge for tours (includes tastings).
Hobart Visitor Information Centre. 20 Davey St. Tel: (03) 6238 4222. www.hobarttravelcentre.com.au. Open: Mon–Fri 8.30am–5.30pm, Sat & Sun 9am–5pm.*

Drive: Hobart to Port Arthur

The drive to Port Arthur on the Tasman Peninsula provides a fascinating mix of stunning coastal scenery and social history. The site of the notorious British penal colony that operated between 1833 and 1855, Port Arthur is now Tasmania's top tourist attraction and a place of beauty that belies its former reputation as 'hell on earth'.

Allow at least a whole day. Total distance: 200km (124 miles) return.

From Hobart, cross the Tasman Bridge and head east on the Tasman Hwy (A3) to Sorrell. From Sorrell, turn right onto the Arthur Hwy (A9), then beyond Dunalley onto the Forestier Peninsula. As you descend into Eaglehawk Neck (21km/13 miles from Hobart), look for signs to the left for Pirates Bay lookout.

1 Pirates Bay lookout and Eaglehawk Neck

On a fine day, the lookout at Pirates Bay is a good introduction to the dramatic coastal scenery of the Tasman Peninsula. Some of the cliffs reach 300m (984ft) in places and are inundated with small bays, arches and caves. The narrow isthmus called Eaglehawk Neck was used in the convict era to prevent escapees from Port Arthur going beyond the peninsula. On the shore below the lookout is the Tessellated Pavement, a platform of square tile-like rocks. *Return to the A9, descend to Eaglehawk Neck and turn left following signs to the Tasman Blowhole.*

2 Blowholes, arches and coastal vistas

A number of dramatic coastal features are accessible from Eaglehawk Neck. Signposted and just a short walk away, they include the Tasman Blowhole, Tasman's Arch and Devil's Kitchen. *Return to the A9 and continue to the Tasmanian Devil Park at Taranna (10km/6 miles).*

3 Tasmanian Devil Park

This park specialises in the care of Tasmanian Devils and is playing an important role in the fight against the cancerous virus (specific to the species) that is decimating the wild population. *Tel: (03) 6250 3230. www.tasmaniandevilpark.com. Open: 9am–5pm. Admission charge. Continue on the A9 to Port Arthur (10km/6 miles).*

4 Port Arthur

Doubtless you will arrive at Port Arthur with a tinge of unease as this was a place of almost unimaginable human suffering. The tour takes several hours and you can either join a guided tour or go it alone. After the tour you can assume a convict identity in the museum, which is both enlightening and entertaining. Evening Historic Ghost Tours are also available.

Arthur Hwy. Tel: (03) 6251 2300/1800 659 101. www.portarthur.org.au. Grounds & ruins open: 8.30am–dusk; visitor centre open: 8.30am–last

Historic Ghost Tour. Admission charge, extra for After Dark Ghost Tour and Bistro Dinner.

5 Coastal walks

There are many excellent coastal walks in the area, and if you intend to stay a while, the half-day walk to **Cape Hauy** is recommended. Ask at the Port Arthur information desk for details (*Port Arthur Historic Site, Arthur Hwy. Tel: (03) 6251 2300. www.portarthur.org.au*). *From the A9, return to Hobart.*

Tasmania

South from Hobart
Bruny Island

At 75km (47 miles) from tip to toe, Bruny Island is a fine day trip with the added incentive of satisfying that strange human desire to reach the tip of any land mass, especially if it has a lighthouse. At **Cape Bruny**, thankfully both the scenery and lighthouse make the trip worth the effort. Along the way is **The Neck**, an isthmus that is little more than 100m (330ft) wide. A boardwalk climbs to the memorable **viewpoint** looking back down its length, and although only seen at dusk, the immediate area is home to dozens of breeding penguins. Other good views of the island's wilderness areas can be found on the unsealed road that threads over the shoulder of the island's highest point, **Mount Mangana** (571m/1,873ft).

Bruny is accessed by car ferry from Kettering. Tel: (03) 6273 6725. www.brunyisland.com.au. Twenty-minute trip, hourly from 6.35am, last ferry 7.50pm (Sun 7pm). There is no public transport on the island. Kettering is 32km (20 miles) south of Hobart.

Hartz Mountains National Park

The Hartz Mountains form an Alpine plateau and part of the eastern border of the Wilderness World Heritage Area. The park is accessed by the snaking (unsealed) Hartz Road (*off Arve Rd*) and there are a number of excellent short or day-long walks with fine views. *24km (15 miles) from Geeveston. www.parks.tas.gov.au*

Huon Valley

To the southwest of Hobart, the Huon River emerges from deep within the

The view looking south over 'The Neck' on Bruny Island

The Air Walk offers exceptional views across the Tahune Forest Reserve

southwest wilderness region to finally empty into the D'Entrecasteaux Channel. The first European settlers were quick to use the valley's fertile soils, with apple growing proving particularly successful.

Huonville, 40km (25 miles) from Hobart, is the largest town in the region and has a full range of facilities. The town's principal attraction is the 35-minute **Huon Jet Boat** ride. The Jet Boat office on the Esplanade doubles as a café and **tourist information centre** (*Tel: (03) 6264 1838. www.huonjet.com. Jet Boat rides (35 mins) 9.15am–4.15pm. Admission charge).*

South of the town, the main highway continues alongside the river, passing through **Franklin**, one of the prettiest of the valley's small towns, before delivering you to **Geeveston**, which was an important timber town back in the 1850s.

Tahune Forest Reserve and the Air Walk

Straddling a stretch of the Huon River and surrounded by mixed, formerly logged, forest, the big attraction of the Tahune Forest Reserve is the Air Walk, the longest of its kind in the world. At around 30m (98ft) in height, the steel walkway extends almost 600m (1,970ft) through the forest canopy to a cantilevered extension and lookout 48m (157ft) above the river. It has just the right amount of wobble and the experience is worthwhile. The **Visitor Centre** includes a café and interpretive area and there are other short walks through the forest. Camping is available.

28km (17 miles) from Geeveston. Via Arve Rd. Tel: (03) 6297 0068. www.forestrytas.com.au. Air Walk open: Apr–Nov 9am–5pm; Dec–Mar 9am–10pm. Admission charge.

The Russell Falls is one of the premier attractions at Mount Field National Park

North from Hobart
The Central Plateau

From New Norfolk (53km/33 miles northwest of Hobart), the **Lyell Highway** (A10) follows the Derwent River Valley then climbs up the Central Plateau on its long and winding route to **Lake St Clair** and (eventually) the west coast. Provided the weather is good, it is one of the most scenic drives in the state. Most people attempt to reach Queenstown in a day, but you may choose to spend a day or two exploring the numerous lakes of the Central Plateau that are legendary for their trout fishing. The largest, **Great Lake**, is especially popular, as the conglomerate of fishing shacks in Miena on its southern shore attests. *168km (104 miles) to Lake St Clair from Hobart.*

Mount Field National Park

Home to the **Russell Falls**, arguably the most famous waterfall in Tasmania, Mount Field National Park is the oldest in Tasmania. Designated in 1917, the park incorporates a diverse variety of habitats, from the windswept rocky Alpine moorland, lakes and tarns (small glacial lakes) that surround Mount Field (1,439m/4,721ft) to the towering gum forests and iconic falls at its base. There are numerous walks, ranging from the 15-minute stroll to the Russell and Horseshoe Falls from the Visitors' Centre, to the more challenging 8-hour summit walk that begins from the terminus of the unsealed road to Lake Dobson and the ski fields (16km/ 10 miles; chains required in winter). Camping (with powered sites) is available near the Visitors' Centre.

80km (50 miles) from Hobart. Tel: (03) 6288 1149. www.parks.tas.gov.au

Richmond

The Georgian village of Richmond is considered one of the prettiest in the state. Built using convict labour, it was once a major stopping point on the way to Port Arthur until the creation of a causeway across the Coal River estuary at Sorrell in 1872 significantly shortened the journey. The main attraction is the much-photographed **sandstone bridge** built in 1823, making it the oldest in Australia. It was also built by convicts, who were kept in appalling conditions, with at least one believed to have committed suicide by throwing himself from the bridge. However, despite its dark history, the bridge gives the modern-day village a distinct English feel and is one of the finest in the country. Also of note is the equally well-preserved **Richmond Gaol**, which housed convicts from 1825 to 1889 (*37 Bathurst St. Tel: (03) 6260 2127. www.richmondvillage.com.au. Open: 9am–5pm. Admission charge*).

The main street plays host to a number of other listed heritage buildings that now house quality galleries, craft shops and eateries. *25km (16 miles) from Hobart.*

Ross

Located on the **Midland Highway** (SH1) between Hobart and Launceston, Ross was, like Richmond, one of the earliest settlements in Tasmania and it too has a **sandstone bridge**. Completed ten years later than the one in Richmond, the bridge incorporates 186 carvings by convict stonemason Daniel Herbert, who was later pardoned – such was the admiration for his work. Other attractions in the town include the remnants of a **Female Factory** site that housed

Tasmania

The picturesque sandstone bridge in Richmond is the oldest in Australia

Tasmania

The beach at Binalong Bay near St Helens

female convicts and their babies between 1848 and 1854, and the **Tasmanian Wool Centre** (*50 Church St. Tel: (03) 6381 5466. www.taswoolcentre.com.au). 100km (62 miles) from Hobart.*

East Coast
Bay of Fires and St Helens
The evocative name of Bay of Fires was bestowed on this coastline by Captain Tobias Furneaux, who joined Cook on his second voyage of discovery in 1773. Furneaux saw a number of fires along the coast, no doubt lit by local Aborigines. Today, the name remains an apt description for this beautiful stretch of coast because it is renowned for its red algae-covered boulders that are in stark contrast to the white sandy beaches. You can walk the entire stretch of coast (12km/7 miles) from Anson's Bay in the southern section of **Mount William National Park** to **The Gardens** (accessed via St Helen's) in the south. If time is short, a day exploring the coast between Binalong Bay and The Gardens

is recommended, particularly around Sloop Lagoon.

St Helens on the George River estuary is an attractive coastal town, popular as a base for fishing, diving and walking. As well as the coastline north of Georges Bay, the beach, dunes and views from **St Helen's Point** are worth exploring.

St Helens is 161km (100 miles) from Launceston.

Bicheno
For both commerce and leisure, Bicheno looks to the sea. It is a base for recreational fishing, and the clear waters provide some of the best **dive sites** in the state. Between autumn and spring, whales, seals and dolphins can also be seen. Another local wildlife attraction is the local **Little Blue Penguin colony** (*Tel: (03) 6375 1333. www.bichenopenguintours.com.au. Admission charge*). Tours are available at dusk when the penguins come ashore to roost.

79km (49 miles) from St Helens.

Freycinet National Park

Freycinet is without doubt one of the most delightful coastal parks in Australia. Named after French explorer Louis de Freycinet in 1800 and 16,900ha (41,760 acres) in size, the park is famous for its idyllic **Wineglass Bay**, a lovely white sandy beach. Yet it doesn't end there. Other dramatic features include the **Hazards**, a series of jagged red and pink granite peaks, **Mount Freycinet** (620m/2,034ft; reached on a two-day walk) and the **Friendly Beaches**. Most settle for a low-level view or walk to Wineglass Bay (1–2 hrs), but for the more energetic, the challenging climb to view the bay from **Mount Amos** (454m/1,489ft) will never be forgotten. Other lovely spots include **Sleepy Bay** and **Cape Tourville**. The area is serviced by the small community of **Coles Bay** at the entrance to the park; it offers all the basic amenities.

125km (78 miles) from Hobart. Tel: (03) 6256 7000. www.parks.tas.gov.au. Admission charge per car.

Maria Island National Park

Maria Island, reached by ferry from Triabunna, has an intriguing mix of social and natural history. A mountainous island, it was first settled as a penal colony in 1825 for convicts whose crimes were of not 'so fragrant a nature'. The island is also renowned for its wildlife, including the Forester kangaroo, Bennett's wallaby and the endangered spotted pardalote (a tiny native bird). There are many fine walks on the island.

Triabunna is 86km (53 miles) from Hobart. For access, tour information & bookings, contact Maria Island Ferry and Ecotours. Tel: (04) 1974 6668. www.mariaislandferry.com.au

Tasmania

Wineglass Bay in the Freycinet National Park is considered one of the world's most picturesque

The other 'hell on earth'

Tasmania is well known for the 'penal' element of its social history, which in its day earned the island the label of 'hell on earth'. However, few are aware that far more heinous crimes were enacted in the early years of settlement, crimes that today would be labelled ethnic cleansing or genocide.

The fate of the Australian Aborigine remains testament to the failure of physical and social integration during the era of European colonisation. Nowhere perhaps was this so tragic – and disgraceful – as in Tasmania.

Four of the last few 'full-blooded' Tasmanian Aborigines, with Truganini on the right, photographed in the 1860s

Aboriginal tribes were present in Tasmania as long as 35,000 years ago. Any other immigrants have only been in Tasmania for just over 200 years. When the British first settled in 1803, an estimated 5–10,000 Aborigines were thought to be distributed throughout the island in nine ethnic groups. Within 30 years that number had been reduced to 300. The biggest killers were virulent diseases such as syphilis and influenza, to which the Aborigines had no immunity. Estimates are unreliable, but research suggests that a minimum of 100 Aborigines were also killed at the hands of the new settlers. Mere mortality rates do not reflect the psychological or physical suffering caused by such displacement together with cultural, familial and spiritual disintegration.

When Lieutenant-Governor George Arthur arrived in Van Diemen's Land in 1824, he implemented two policies to deal with the growing conflict between settlers and the Aborigines. First, bounties were awarded for the capture of Aborigines and, second, Arthur tried to improve relations by luring Aborigines into camps.

Captain Cook landing in Tasmania in 1777

Cove, south of Hobart. By 1860, there were about a dozen left and the last known survivor – reputed to be Truganini, the daughter of the chief of the Bruny Island people – died in 1873, aged 64.

In many ways, the memory of Truganini is celebrated as a testament to the suffering of her people. Before she was 18, her mother had been killed by whalers; her first fiancé died after having his hands cut off while saving her from abduction; and, in 1828, her two sisters were abducted and taken to Kangaroo Island and sold as slaves. Truganini married, but her husband died when she was still in her twenties. Despite this, she was not only wise in spirit and strong of character, but late in life could still enjoy a laugh with the 'white fella'.

In 1997, a Statement of Apology (specific to the removal of Aboriginal children) was issued – supported by the Tasmanian Parliament – with the wording:

'That this house, on behalf of all Tasmanian(s)... expresses its deep and sincere regret at the hurt and distress caused by past policies under which Aboriginal children were removed from their families and homes; apologises to the Aboriginal people for those past actions and reaffirms its support for reconciliation between all Australians.'

In 1833, the Christian missionary George Robertson persuaded all the remaining 300 'full-blooded' Aborigines that were not being used as slave labour to be translocated to Flinders Island off the northeast Tasmanian coast. Left to their own devices, a lack of resources and poor conditions led to the death of 250 Aborigines within 14 years. In 1847, the 50 or so remaining Aborigines were relocated, this time to Oyster

Tasmania

Devonport, Launceston and environs

Deloraine

Considered the arts hub of the north, this rural town has some good galleries and a pleasant down-to-earth atmosphere. It is often used as a base from which to explore the **Great Western Tiers**, with the half-day trip to the **Liffey Falls** (35km/22 miles) or **Mole Creek** karst (limestone) caves the most popular (*Tel: (03) 6363 5182. www.parks.tas.gov.au. Open: 10am–4pm. Admission charge*). The intricately crafted **Yarns artwork** (quilt) depicting all aspects of the Meander Valley hangs in the Deloraine **visitor information centre** (*98 Emu Bay Rd. Tel: (03) 6362 3471. www.greatwesterntiers.net.au*). It took 300 people over 10,000 hours and 18 months to complete (*Admission charge*).
Deloraine is 49km (30 miles) from Devonport.

Devonport

The arrival point for the *Spirit of Tasmania* ferry: stock up here on information and supplies before setting forth on your Tasmanian adventure. There are not many specific attractions in Devonport, but a visit to **Mersey Bluff** is the best bet.
Devonport is 277km (172 miles) from Hobart; 100km (62 miles) from Launceston. The visitor information centre supplies information for the whole state. Directly opposite the ferry terminal on the opposite side of the river,

One of many murals that decorate the small rural town of Sheffield

92 Formby Rd. Tel: (03) 6424 4466. www.devonporttasmania.travel. Open: 7.30am–last ferry sailing.

Launceston

Established in 1805 and now with a population of around 70,000, Launceston is Tasmania's second-largest city. Sited at the head of the Tamar River, mining was a staple industry before tourism began to play an important role. The city is renowned for its heritage architecture, with the post office and the Town Hall surrounding Civic Square being two fine examples. The **Queen Victoria Museum and Art Gallery** has a colonial art collection and tells the tale of that now extinct icon of the state, the Thylacine (Tasmanian Tiger). It is split between two venues (*Invermay Rd, Inveresk; Wellington St, Royal Park. Tel: (03) 6323 3777. www.qvmag.tas.gov.au. Open: 10am–5pm. Free admission*).

To the east of the city centre, **Cataract Gorge** with its surrounding parklands and a chairlift offers scenery that is especially dramatic when the River Esk is in flood.

Launceston is 198km (123 miles) from Hobart. Visitor Information Centre. Cornwall Square, 12–16 St John St. Tel: 1800 651 827.
www.visitlauncestontamar.com.au

Sheffield

The small rural town of Sheffield, between Devonport and Cradle Mountain, is renowned for its **murals** depicting mainly pioneering history and adorning various façades throughout its centre.
30km (19 miles) from Devonport.

Tamar Valley

The Tamar Valley, to the north of Launceston, is a region of both serenity and danger. The area offers a pleasant scenic drive alongside the broad river, with various points of interest and a growing number of **vineyards** with cellar doors. The small mining town of **Beaconsfield** was established during the gold rush in 1869 but is better known for a mining accident in 2006, when locals Todd Russell and Brant Webb survived 14 days trapped underground.

Tasmania

A view of First Basin at Cataract Gorge

Tour: Northwest coast

Lacking any high-profile attractions and a main road connection to the West Coast townships, the far northwest corner of the state is often left off the travelling agenda, but this is precisely its appeal. Here you can get off the beaten track in one of the most unspoilt areas of the state.

Allow 2 days. Total distance: approximately 250km (155 miles).

Start from Burnie, 50km (31 miles) west of Devonport on the Bass Hwy (SH1).

1 Burnie

First established as an agricultural town and failing due to poor soils and climate,

Burnie reinvented itself as a port serving the tin and timber industry and is now the state's fourth-largest town. Local attractions include the **Emu Valley Rhododendron Gardens** (*South via B18, Breffny Rd. Tel: (03) 6431 6505*).

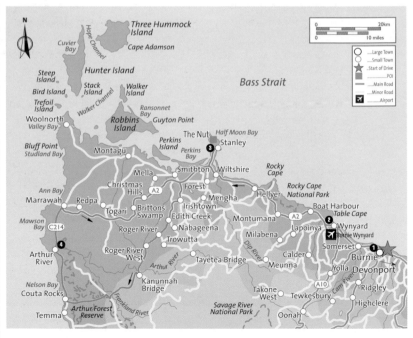

www.emuvalleyrhodo.com.au. Open: Aug–Feb 10am–4pm. Admission charge) and the **Lactos Cheese Factory** (145 Old Surrey Rd. Tel: (03) 6431 2566. Open: Mon–Fri 9am–5pm, Sat & Sun 10am–4pm. Free admission). You can also try your hand at papermaking at **Creative Paper** (2 Bass Hwy. Tel: (03) 6430 5831. www.creativepapertas.com.au. Open: 9am–5pm. Admission charge). Burnie Visitor Information Centre, Little Alexander St. Tel: (03) 6434 6111. www.discovertasmania.com.

From Burnie, continue west on the Bass Hwy (now called the A2) to Wynyard.

2 Wynyard

Set on the banks of the Inglis River and in the shadow of the aptly named **Table Cape**, the small village of Wynyard is renowned for its tulip festival held every October (www.bloomintulips.com.au). During this brief period almost the entire plateau of the cape, which is in essence one huge tulip farm, becomes awash with colour (Table Cape Rd then Lighthouse Rd. Tel: (03) 6442 2012. Open: In season (Oct)). Even without the tulips, the views from the Cape and lighthouse are worth investigating.

From Wynyard, continue west on the Bass Hwy (A2) to the Stanley turn-off (right, 53km/33 miles).

3 Stanley

Most famous for its 152m (499ft) volcanic lump, known as '**The Nut**', Stanley draws people from miles around and has done so since it was

The northwest coast near Couta Rocks

established as the base for the Van Diemen's Land Company (VDL) in 1825. Today, as well as the views of and from its plateau (reached by foot or by chairlift from Browns Road), the village itself has much character. Book at the visitor information centre (45 Main Rd. Tel: (03) 6458 1330. www.stanley.com.au).

Back on the A2, continue west. 2km (1¼ miles) before Smithton follow signs (left) to Arthur Forest Reserve (via Irishtown and Edith Creek). You will need a detailed map to reach the west coast (Couta Rocks) through the forest and to return (north) to the A2 via Arthur River.

4 Arthur Forest Reserve and Arthur River

This scenic drive takes you to various viewpoints and picnic spots through the forest and beside the Arthur River before delivering you at the west coast and Couta Rocks (Tel: (03) 6457 1158. www.arthurrivercruises.com). West Point (accessed just before the A2) is another spot well worth a look.

At the junction with the A2, return east via Smithton to Burnie (144km/89 miles).

You little devil

Among its many characteristics, the Tasmanian Devil lets off an offensive odour when stressed, has an extremely loud and disturbing screech, and plenty of attitude. It can be vicious when feeding and is known to both hunt prey and scavenge, usually at night. Although it is mainly solitary, it sometimes eats with other devils. Sexual activity takes place regularly, often loudly, both day and night, and males often fight over females. Well, although the likeness is uncanny, this description belongs not to that common creature the human teenager, but to the endangered 'devil', as in Tasmanian – the only carnivorous marsupial on earth. Black in colour and about the size of a small dog, stockily built and with hind legs slightly shorter than the fore, it is not entirely dissimilar in stature to the African hyena.

Tasmanian Devils – or *Sarcophilus harrisii*, to give them their proper name – were expatriated from the Australian mainland during the last ice age 10,000 years ago. Ideally suited to the Tasmanian habitat, they flourished until the Europeans arrived with their notorious 'if it moves shoot it' hunting policy, practised wholesale in the name of both the Empire and any introduced livestock. Thankfully, unlike its only close relation, the Thylacine (Tasmanian Tiger), or the entire population of Tasmanian Aborigines, *harrisii* survived and since 1941 has been fully protected.

Now, had it not been for Warner Bros., few would be aware of the little devil's existence, let alone care. However, due to that cursing, whirlwind troublemaker 'Taz', the famous Looney Tunes cartoon character, everyone loves the 'devil'. Tourism Tasmania certainly do, and you will find many wildlife sanctuaries throughout the state that promise you an encounter and a happy snap, especially at feeding time. The pups are actually quite adorable, even if

The Tasmanian Devil is an endangered species

The marsupial can let off an offensive smell

fighting. It is fatal and particularly worrying because the devil's immune system does not apparently recognise the cancer cells as foreign and so it spreads rapidly, resulting in starvation and death.

Faced with possible extinction, massive efforts have been made to protect and isolate healthy animals, with some even being captured and transported to zoos on the mainland. Research has also been intensive.

Hopefully, with human help, just as nature created the problem it may also fix it, provided the wild population can develop immunity. Only time will tell. In the meantime it seems that on this occasion even the devil needs an angel – and a miracle.

you wouldn't dare pick up Mum and Dad if they were hitchhiking.

So, despite their early brush with human invaders, you could argue that devils would now be quite happy with their lot. But sadly, on the contrary, the poor creatures are currently at war with nature and themselves, not humans. Since it was first diagnosed in 1996, a fatal disease called Devil Facial Tumour Disease (DFTD) has decimated numbers by up to 50 per cent and has spread across half the state. It is a transmissible, particularly aggressive parasitic cancer appearing initially around the face and passed on physically, most often during

The little devil immortalised in art

The World Heritage Parks

The Tasmanian Wilderness World Heritage Area (WHA) covers 13,838sq km (5,342sq miles) – about one-fifth of the state – and contains some of the most pristine natural habitats on earth. Facing considerable threat and having survived some hard-fought battles, it is a wilderness held dear to most Tasmanians and for the visitor a wonderland of superb scenery and outdoor activity.

For detailed parks information, visit the accredited visitor information centres, Tasmanian Parks and Wildlife Service park centres. www.parks.tas.gov.au. Ask for copies of the 'Tasmania's 60 Great Short Walks' and 'National Parks, Forest and Waterways Tasmania Visitor Guide' brochures from the above.

Cradle Mountain on a clear day

Cradle Mountain and Lake St Clair National Park

The vast 161,200ha (398,320-acre) Cradle Mountain and Lake St Clair National Park is the most visited and best known of all Tasmania's parks. With its iconic yet illusive mountain to the fore, the primary access point is from the north. Here, the **Overland Track** begins its 80km (50-mile) route through the peaks, Alpine plains and forests of the glacier-carved landscape to Lake St Clair.

For many, it is enough to take a stroll around **Lake Dove**, set like a reflective welcome mat below the jagged ridge of the Cradle, enough to see, with luck, the mountain minus its cloak of cloud

cast asunder at sunset. However, whether passive or active, a trip to Cradle Mountain is without doubt a Tasmanian 'must-see'.

91km (57 miles) from Devonport. For access and information, see p122.

Franklin-Gordon Rivers National Park

For many conservationists the world over, the words 'Franklin' and 'Gordon' are like 'Bannockburn' or 'Gallipoli', forever remembered and revered as the site of battles as worthy as life itself. Were it not for the actions of a dedicated few like Tasmanian photographer Peter Dombrovskis and

the then Tasmanian Wilderness Society director Bob Brown (now head of Australia's Green Party), much of this park would now be underwater and powering the light bulbs of the nation. They managed to advertise the cause – one that would become Australia's largest conservation battle of the 1980s – and the battle began to save the Franklin from the Hydro Tasmania proposed hydroelectric power scheme, the Franklin Dam. Much of the 4,463sq km (1,723sq mile) park is inaccessible, but its awe-inspiring beauty can still be witnessed along the Gordon River and Scotts Peak Road west of Hobart, at the Lyell Highway between Derwent Bridge and Queenstown, or by river cruise from Strahan. Weather plays an important role, but if you put all three of these trips on your travel agenda, chances are you will get lucky.
117km (73 miles) west of Hobart.

Southwest National Park
The 6,052sq km (2,337sq mile) Southwest National Park is real 'tiger country', and Tasmania's most remote. Like New Zealand's Fiordland, there are many places here that have never seen a human being. For the visitor short of time, a day's walk to South East Cape (the southernmost tip of Australia) from Cockle Creek 148km (92 miles) south of Hobart is recommended, or alternatively a scenic flight from Hobart to Melaleuca – the access point for the 80km (50-mile) South Coast Track.
93km (58 miles) west of Hobart.

Lake Pedder in the remote Southwest National Park

Walk: Cradle Mountain

Cradle Mountain is the Uluru of Tasmania. Not rounded but jagged; higher, younger and colder; and – given the weather in these parts – far more elusive.

There are many walks on offer within the Cradle Mountain area, with the best known being the 80km (50-mile) multi-day Overland Track between Lake Dove and Lake St Clair.

The following circuit around Lake Dove is a moderate, 6km (4-mile) 2-hour walk offering the best low-level views of the mountain, with the option of ascending the peak, should fitness and conditions allow.

Start the walk at Lake Dove.

Note: Weather conditions can change dramatically for the worse, even in summer, so take warm clothing and appropriate footwear, and always go prepared.

1 Lake Dove

Start your walk at sunrise on the shores and natural amphitheatre of the glacial Lake Dove. It is only a short walk from the car park to the lake's edge, where you may be lucky and secure that elusive reflection of the mountain.

From the shores of the lake, head in a clockwise direction following the boardwalk for 100m (110yds).

Lake Dove marks the start of many walks, with one of the most popular being the ascent of the iconic Cradle Mountain

Cradle Mountain at dawn

2 Lookout Rock

A large boulder accessed just off the boardwalk offers an elevated position for viewing and photographing the mountain with the lake below. *From Lookout Rock, continue around the lake.*

3 The Boatshed

Near the completion of the circuit track, the small boatshed offers another good photo opportunity.

Extended options

There are several sidetracks that access the higher elevations and natural features that include Alpine lakes, ridges and viewpoints. The 1,545m (5,069ft) summit of Cradle Mountain (600m/1969ft above the car park) is also an option. The main track heads west, via Lake Lilla, ascending the ridge to Marion's Lookout, before heading south to Kitchen Hut and the Cradle Mountain summit track. Alternatively,

you climb up (or down) from Lake Dove via Lake Wilks (*southern edge of Lake Dove*), or via Hanson's Peak (*northeast edge of Lake Dove*). The summit walk will take from 6–8 hours.

Practicalities

The Parks Tasmania Cradle Mountain Visitor Centre is located at the entrance to the park (*Cradle Mountain Rd. Tel: (03) 6492 1110. www.parks.tas.gov.au. Admission charge per vehicle*).

Lake Dove car park (*8km/5 miles from the visitor centre*) can be accessed by car, foot or shuttle bus (*Admission charge*).

There are various accommodation options from lodge and cabin to motor park and campsite, but all are expensive (*see pp138–9*).

Most of the establishments have eateries that are open to the public, and shops selling souvenirs and basic supplies. There is also a shop and café 3km (2 miles) before the park entrance at the shuttle terminal and Cradle Mountain Visitor Centre.

Cradle Mountain lies at the northern end of the Cradle Mountain and Lake St Clair National Park. It is 1½ hours from Devonport via the B19 and B14 south to Sheffield, then the C136 and C132 to the park entrance. From the west, drive 2 hours along the A10 and C132 from Queenstown or 1½ hours from Burnie via the B18 through Ridgley, then the A10 and C132 to reach the park.

Strahan and the West Coast

Queenstown

Amid such beauty, Queenstown is unfortunately not so photogenic. The bare hills scattered by the 'headstone' roots and stumps of former forest giants are now almost an icon and a tourist attraction in themselves, but more for the shake of the head than a picture postcard. They are the result of the former activities of the local copper, silver and gold mining industry that began in the 1800s, stripping the native forest to feed the furnaces of the copper smelters, with the by-product of sulphurous fumes and erosion preventing regrowth. Efforts are being made to replace the topsoil but progress is slow.

However, Queenstown is a supply stop and the home of the far more attractive **West Coast Wilderness Railway**. Without doubt the town's saving grace, the much-loved steam engine puffs and fusses its way along the 1896-vintage 34km (21-mile) rack-and-pinion line to Strahan, via the bush-clad valleys and hills that the mining companies never reached (*Tel: 1800 628 288. www.puretasmania.com.au. Departs Queenstown station 10am & 3pm; arrives Strahan 2.45pm & 7pm (coach transfer back to Queenstown departs 4pm arriving 4.45pm, & 8pm arriving 8.45pm. Admission charge).*
Queenstown is 88km (55 miles) from Derwent Bridge.

Strahan

Due to its remote location, Strahan (*pronounced straw-n*) was not properly settled until the 1870s, when hardy

An old steam engine is readied for action on the Wilderness Railway between Queenstown and Strahan

Strahan, on the west coast of Tasmania

pioneers arrived to plunder the region's rich natural resources. At first it was a staging post for the notorious Sarah Island (Macquarie Harbour) penal colony, established in 1822, before developing as a port for local mining concerns and a small fishing fleet. Strahan was also a base for bush lumberjacks, or 'piners', extracting the much-prized Huon Pine. With the extraction of natural resources largely over, the town's principal raison d'être is tourism, with the two major draws being a leisurely scenic cruise up the Franklin and Gordon 'wilderness' rivers and the scenic West Coast Wilderness Railway from Queenstown (*see opposite*). There are numerous river cruise options, and other aquatic-based activities include jet boating, fishing and kayaking. Scenic flights are available by seaplane. Competition for the tourist dollar is fierce so you are advised to shop around. The visitor information centre is a good place to start.

If a little solitude and wild scenery are in order, then Ocean Beach, at the mouth of Macquarie Harbour, is a good escape. There you can view the tumultuous tidal outlet known as Hell's Gate and walk the beach in search of interesting flotsam and jetsam. The beach stretches 36km (22 miles) north, making it the longest in the state. Henty Dunes, 10km (6 miles) north of Strahan, offer another fine milieu.
40km (25 miles) from Queenstown. Strahan Visitor Information Centre. The Esplanade. Tel: (03) 6472 6800. www.westcoast.tas.gov.au. Open: summer 10am–7pm; winter 10am–6pm.

Getting away from it all

Given the sheer size of Australia and the fact that around 85 per cent of the population live in cities or coastal towns, it is not difficult to get away from the crowds. You could throw caution to the wind, buy a map, pick a road and follow your nose. As long as you go prepared, Australia has much to offer but, given the time constraints, most travellers stick to a tight agenda. By far the best getaway venues are the nation's national parks, with their spectacular landscapes and diverse flora and fauna.

New South Wales alone has about 600 parks, with the vast majority on or within easy reach of the coast. Victoria too has its fair share, with some national gems like the celebrated Wilson's Promontory. In Tasmania, the word 'park' is often prefixed with the title 'World Heritage', which means you are in for something special.

COASTAL NATIONAL PARKS

The following is a sample of the best coastal national parks in the southeast, but it is by no means a comprehensive list. For detailed information, contact the following parks services.
New South Wales National Parks and Wildlife Service (NPWS). *Tel: 1300 361 967. www.nationalparks.nsw.gov.au*
South Australia National Parks and Wildlife (SA). *Tel: (08) 8336 0924. www.parks.sa.gov.au*
Note that almost all parks charge a vehicle day-use admission fee, and separate camping fees apply. Annual or multi-day passes are recommended.

Tasmania Tasmania Parks and Wildlife Service. *Tel: 1300 135 513. www.parks.tas.gov.au*
Victoria Parks Victoria. *Tel: 131 963. www.parkweb.vic.gov.au*

New South Wales
Ben Boyd National Park
The park (10,486ha/25,911 acres) is named after Benjamin Boyd, a prominent 19th-century entrepreneur. The rugged coastline is renowned for its colourful geological features and historic lighthouses. Two must-see venues are the 'Pinnacles' and Green Cape light station, where you can stay overnight in keepers' cottages. There are excellent, quiet campsites. You can go on walks from 1–30km (2/3 mile–19 miles).
23km (14 miles) south of Eden. Tel: (02) 6495 5000 (see p47).

Booderee National Park
Taking up most of the Bherwerre Peninsula, on the southern foreshore

of picturesque Jervis Bay, Booderee (6,300ha/15,567 acres) encompasses a wide range of coastal habitats and is home to a number of endangered species, including the Bristle bird. The park is renowned for its pristine white sandy beaches. There are numerous fine walking tracks, and excellent (but expensive) camping is available.
12km (7 miles) south of Nowra.
Tel: (02) 4443 0977 (see p44).

Mimosa Rocks National Park
Rugged coastal headlands, cliffs and rock stacks are the main features here, backed by mature native bush rich in wildlife. The park (5,802ha/ 14,337 acres) is a great overnight camping spot on the way south from Sydney, particularly at Aragunnu in the northern area. There are basic facilities and firewood is supplied. Short walk opportunities.
20km (12 miles) south of Bermagui.
Tel: (02) 4476 2888.

NEW SOUTH WALES SOUTH COAST AND SNOWY MOUNTAINS CAMPSITES
Aragunnu campsite, Mimosa Rocks National Park (Bermagui).
Bittangabee campsite, Ben Boyd National Park (Eden).
Green Patch camping area, Booderee National Park (Jervis Bay).
Pebbly Beach campsite, Murramarang National Park (Bateman's Bay).
Thredbo Diggings (Alpine Way), Kosciuszko National Park (Jindabyne).

Getting away from it all

Wave watching in Ben Boyd National Park

Getting away from it all

The lush rainforest of Great Otway National Park

Murramarang National Park

Murramarang (12,387ha/30,608 acres) is similar to Mimosa Rocks and famous for its tame (but wild) mob of Eastern Grey kangaroos. Excellent camping is available, particularly at Pebbly Beach. There are basic facilities and firewood is supplied. There are short and day-long walk opportunities.

10km (6 miles) north of Bateman's Bay. Tel: (02) 4478 6582 (see p45).

South Australia
Coorong National Park

A landscape of dune systems, lagoons and wetlands along the narrow 150km (93-mile) long Younghusband Peninsula. The park (50,000ha/ 123,548 acres) is rich in birdlife. There are many walking trails from 1–27km (²/₃ mile–17 miles), and numerous good campsites.

156km (97 miles) southeast of Adelaide. Tel: (08) 8575 1200.

Tasmania
Freycinet National Park

This is Tasmania's premier coastal national park (16,900ha/41,760 acres), which is saying something! The main attraction is Wineglass Bay, often lauded as one of the prettiest beaches in the world. Mountainous in parts, there are several superb viewpoints and walks ranging from 1–30km (²/₃ mile–19 miles). There are three campsites within the park and a motor park in the village of Coles Bay at the entrance to the park.

125km (78 miles) northeast of Hobart. Tel: (03) 6256 7000 (see p111).

Victoria
Great Otway National Park

Renowned for its diverse range of landscapes and vegetation types, the park (10,300ha/25,451 acres) has a wide range of walking options from 1–5km (²/₃ mile–3 miles), with many venturing to waterfalls or quiet beaches. Koala spotting is also popular and there are many good camping areas.

162km (101 miles) southwest of Melbourne. Tel: (03) 5237 6529.

Wilson's Promontory National Park

The southernmost point of the Australian mainland and Victoria's premier coastal national park, Wilson's Promontory covers 9,000ha (22,239 acres). Remote and dramatic coastal aesthetics, abundant wildlife and many short, day-long and multi-day walking options, including the popular 37km

(23-mile) hike to the 1859 lighthouse and the 3.4km (2-mile) ascent of Mount Oberon. There are over 450 camping and caravan sites, but it needs it! Book well ahead.

157km (98 miles) southeast of Melbourne. Tel: 131 963/(03) 8627 4700 (see pp50–51).

INLAND NATIONAL PARKS
New South Wales
Morton National Park

There are echoes of the Blue Mountains here, with sandstone escarpments dotted with viewpoints and towering waterfalls, including the 82m (269ft) Fitzroy Falls. There is a modern visitor centre near the Fitzroy Falls and vocal lyrebirds frequent the immediate area. There are several short walks to and around the viewpoints throughout the park. The park (190,747ha/ 471,329 acres) is best accessed via the

Little Oberon Bay, Wilson's Promontory National Park

road that passes through the pretty village of Kangaroo Valley, northwest of Nowra (New South Wales south coast). It is a scenic drive.

150km (93 miles) south of Sydney. Tel: (02) 4887 7270.

Tasmania
Walls of Jerusalem National Park

The evocatively named Walls of Jerusalem National Park (51,800ha/ 128,000 acres) sits adjacent to and east of the Cradle Mountain and Lake St Clair National Park. A high plateau with high rainfall, it contains over 4,000 lakes and tarns. It is best experienced from the fringes, especially via Mole Creek south of Devonport.

90km (56 miles) south of Devonport.

Victoria
Grampians National Park

With over 1 million visitors a year, the Grampians (170,000ha/420,064 acres) is Victoria's most popular inland national park (without skis). An ancient and rugged landscape of bush-clad escarpments attracts rock climbers, bushwalkers or those just searching for dramatic views. Severe fires swept through the park in 2006 but the regeneration has become an attraction in itself. There are numerous good short or extended walking opportunities and good camping. The park is best accessed via Halls Gap (Western Highway), home to the visitor centre.

260km (162 miles) west of Melbourne. Tel: (03) 5361 4000.

Bush fires in Australia

In the age of a mass media so driven by sensationalism, many are unaware that the phenomenon of bush fires across the world's driest continent is as natural as the lightning that ignites them. Bush fires can have a huge environmental impact and pose a significant threat to both life and property, but with something so natural, why so much drama?

Fire has always played a fundamental role in the ecology of the Australian environment, with many native plants relying on it for reproduction. Furthermore, the Aborigines have, for thousands of years, used fire to hunt animals in arguably the earliest form of land management practice. Although there is much debate as to how those practices altered the ecosystem

A bush fire rages on Tasmania's east coast

and promoted fire-loving species, the fact remains that bush fires are nothing new. So why is it that now, every summer, the populated areas of Australia, particularly in the south and east, have to brace themselves for the worst? Why does the worst so often happen, and is it all going terribly wrong?

Two main factors seem to be at play. First, there is an increased incidence of drought through climate change, and, second, human beings are now present (in ever-increasing numbers) within areas susceptible to fire. Beyond that, sadly, the problem is arson or accident (often cigarette ends), and simply another link in the chain of environmental destruction that has come about in Australia due to the impact and pace of human invasion.

In the last 200 years, much of the Australian landscape has been altered beyond recognition, often in the name of entirely inappropriate agricultural and industrial land practices. Where we felt we could graze sheep we did so, where there were trees we cut them down, where resources were found we plundered them. The result is a landscape that is, over vast areas, unnatural, and as

Fire devastation in Flinders Ranges National Park, near the Remarkable Rocks

long as there is fuel to feed it, fire does not care.

The worst bush fires are usually labelled as 'Black' followed by the day on which they occurred. The worst event so far was February 2009's 'Black Saturday' in Victoria, with the loss of 173 lives, over 2,000 homes and 450,000ha (1.1 million acres) of bush burned across the east of the state. Others included Black Friday, 13 January 1939, when over 2 million ha (4,942,000 acres) of land were burned across Victoria, with the loss of 71 lives. Several towns were entirely destroyed. The Royal Commission into the fires noted, 'it appeared the whole State was alight on Friday, 13 January, 1939'. On Black Tuesday, 7 February 1967, over 110 separate fire fronts burned through

some 264,200ha (653,000 acres) of land in southern Tasmania within the space of five hours, with the loss of 62 lives.

On Ash Wednesday, 16 February 1983, again in Victoria and South Australia, 75 lives were lost. During the season of 2006–7, fires raged in almost every state, or 'wherever a hot north wind was blowing', with few lives lost but a staggering 1 million ha (2½ million acres) burned in Victoria alone.

Few would disagree that the incidence of bush fire in Australia is increasing, or that it goes hand in hand with the occurrence of drought exacerbated by climate change. The big debate is how land should be conserved, developed and, above all, managed in the light of these facts.

When to go

Given the size and geographical position of Southeast Australia, some of its appeal is that at any time of year part of it always offers the ideal outdoor climate. Sydney and Melbourne are two of the most happening cities on earth and inevitably they play a leading role in any visit, but they are supported admirably by the other state capitals of Canberra, Adelaide and Hobart, where there is plenty going on all year round, from festivals to local markets.

Climate and weather

You are probably not coming to Australia to dance in the rain, snowboard or snuggle up by an open fire (although you can do all three). Instead, you will be intent on hitting the beach armed with little except your best bikini or pair of surf shorts, shades and sunblock.

You are almost guaranteed lots of sun and perfect temperatures, but Australia can surprise with some dramatic weather – at any time of year. The Southeast can see wild weather events with damaging storms (particularly in summer), floods, and some eyebrow-raising temperatures.

Being a southern hemisphere continent, Australia's seasons are the opposite of those in the northern hemisphere, and this is usually part of the attraction. Broadly speaking, the peak summer season between Sydney and Adelaide is from the middle of November through to the end of February. Temperatures at this time are generally in the mid 20s°C to low 30s°C (high 70s°F to high 80s°F), and clear sunny days the norm. Depending on wind direction, temperatures – particularly in Victoria and South Australia – can soar to the low 40s°C (low 100s°F) or drop dramatically in just a few hours, earning Melbourne the label of having 'four seasons in one day'.

Given the ocean influence and southerly aspect, Tasmania gets a lot

It's not always sunny on the East Coast of Australia

more 'weather' generally, so the more time spent there the better your chances are of seeing what you want to.

When planning a long trip to the southeast, say three months or more, try to make spring or autumn the core of your visit.

Events, domestic and school holidays

Australia hosts many internationally significant events of all types and sizes and the ongoing list of domestic and regional events is vast. From sport to fashion and music to art, there is always plenty happening, especially in the main centres and state capitals of Sydney, Melbourne, Canberra, Adelaide and Hobart. You may be visiting Australia to attend a specific event or to coincide your travels with others, but you will never be short of choice, particularly in summer.

Australians are notorious for their enviable lifestyle, so bear in mind that when it comes to getting out there and enjoying yourself, the foreign visitor is often in the minority, especially in summer and school holidays. Between 24 December and February, you can just about forget the nine-to-five modus operandi. At this time, almost everybody heads to the beach, so book all accommodation and activities well in advance. Other school holidays include a week or two around Easter, two weeks in June and July, and another couple of weeks during September and October.

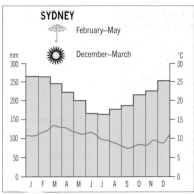

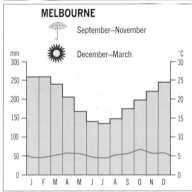

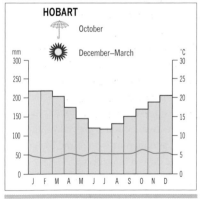

WEATHER CONVERSION CHART

25.4mm = 1 inch

$°F = 1.8 \times °C + 32$

Getting around

The best way to see the southeast is independently, using a hired vehicle (usually a campervan) or for longer visits buying one second-hand. The latter does present its own dangers, but because so many people choose this option, Sydney and the main centres are well geared to sales and, with care, you can certainly secure a reliable bargain and sell it again before departure.

If time is short and you want to cover a lot of ground, you may have to be more specific about your itinerary, focus on only a few locations, and combine domestic air travel with short-term vehicle hire. This option is becoming increasingly popular given the competitive prices of domestic flights currently available and car hire in the main centres.

There is an overnight ferry to Tasmania from Melbourne. However, you can buy a flight from Melbourne to Hobart or Launceston quite cheaply one-way, so vehicle hire once you get there may be an alternative.

Public transport in all of the states is based on a variety of air, bus, ferry and train networks, and is generally quite good, although in Sydney and Melbourne delays should be expected. Details of trains, bus and ferry services can be found in the *Thomas Cook Overseas Timetable*, available to buy online from *www.thomascookpublishing.com*, Thomas Cook branches in the UK or *tel: 01733 416477.*

By air

Sydney, Melbourne, Canberra, Adelaide and Hobart all have an international airport. There are four main domestic carriers so prices are very competitive. **Jetstar** *Tel: 131 538. www.jetstar.com.au* **Qantas** *Tel: 131 313.* *www.qantas.com.au* **Tiger** *Tel: (03) 9335 3033.* *www.tigerairways.com* **Virgin Blue** *Tel: 136 789.* *www.virginblue.com.au*

The best and cheapest way is to book well in advance and on the Internet. There are also several regional airways operating smaller planes on specialist routes. For up-to-date information, contact your destination's tourist office.

By bus

The interstate bus services provide a viable way to move up and down the coast but, given the distances involved, it can prove uncomfortable. **Greyhound** (*Tel: 1300 473 946.* *www.greyhound.com.au*) and **Premier**

Motor Services (*Tel: 133 410. www.premierms.com.au*) are the main players. Their network follows all the main interstate highways with offshoots including the Blue Mountains and Canberra. As well as scheduled routes and fares, they offer jump-on, jump-off passes.

There are many other smaller regional companies, so for information contact the relevant visitor information centre. **Countrylink** (*Tel: 132 232. www.countrylink.nsw.gov.au*) in New South Wales and **V-Line** (*Tel: 136 196. www.vline.com.au*) in Victoria also have coach services to some centres in conjunction with rail schedules.

By car or campervan

Given the size of Australia, car hire is usually reserved for city and regional travel; the long haul is the domain of the almost iconic campervan. In summer, the main highways along the coast are awash with them, and they are not just used by foreign visitors. Many Australians (especially retirees or 'Grey Nomads', as they are dubbed) have campervans, camper trailers (in essence a tent on wheels) and the ubiquitous 'Jayco' caravans.

If you live in a small, heavily populated country, travelling by vehicle in Australia will be an enlightening experience. Distances are great and travelling times between the major cities, towns and sights long. Yet instead of becoming bored and fighting the odometer, relax and make driving part of the whole holiday experience.

If you are travelling for more than three months, consider buying a car or a van, or hiring a campervan. Roads are generally in good condition and sealed,

Getting around

Trams still form a major mode of transport in Melbourne

The *Spirit of Tasmania* ferry as seen from the main street in Devonport

with only back roads (especially within the national parks) requiring 4WD. If you intend to do some off-road driving, see a bit of the outback, or want to investigate the national parks fully, you should hire a 4WD campervan, but it will cost more. Always check with the hire company where you can and cannot take your 4WD vehicle (some will not allow them off graded roads or on sand), and your liability in the case of an accident.

There are numerous hire companies in Australia and you are advised to shop around for the best deal. Campervan models vary from the basic two-berth van to the travelling family palace. The main companies are **Britz** (*Tel: 1800 331 454. www.britz.com.au*) and **Maui** (*Tel: 1300 363 800. www.maui.com.au*). Standard vehicles can be hired in the main centres and all the major international companies are present. It is worth looking at smaller companies as they often offer great deals, but as with any hire agreement always read the small print.

Fuel costs

Fuel costs are generally favourable in comparison to the UK or USA, but like most places they are rising rapidly. Unleaded can be up to 15 per cent more expensive outside the main cities. Diesel is currently more expensive than unleaded, but it is less prone to price fluctuations. With the distances involved, when it comes to budgeting

you will find fuel expenses exceed those of food and rival those of accommodation. On long journeys, follow the standard rules for minimising costs: ensure you have correct tyre pressures, avoid using air conditioning if possible, check the oil regularly, stick to 90–100kph (56–62mph), and, of course, try to hunt out the cheapest fuel! A trip between Sydney and Adelaide taking in Tasmania can easily involve driving 15,000+ km (9,300 miles). Choosing an economical vehicle and conserving fuel can save a lot of money.

By train

Given the price and convenience of domestic flights, train travel between the main centres is usually the domain of the enthusiast, but it remains a viable mode of transport. One trip worth considering is a jaunt into the outback from Sydney to Adelaide on the *Indian Pacific*. Routes are operated by **Great Southern Railway** (*Tel: 132 147. www.gsr.com.au*). In New South Wales **Countrylink** (*Tel: 132 232. www.countrylink.info*) offers rail and rail/coach services state-wide, while in Victoria it is **V-Line** (*Tel: 136 196. www.vline.com.au*). In Sydney and Melbourne, metro train services are linked to bus and ferry networks and this is an excellent way of negotiating the city. In Sydney, contact **CityRail** (*Tel: 131 500. www.cityrail.info*), and in Melbourne, **Metlink** (*Tel: 131 638. www.metlinkmelbourne.com.au*).

Accommodation

Southeast Australia offers a range of accommodation options to suit all budgets, from cheap national park campsites to exclusive and luxurious resorts. Regardless of budget there is rarely a problem finding a clean, comfortable bed anywhere, but during high season you are advised to book all accommodation well in advance. The local visitor information centres can supply full listings and book on your behalf.

The climate in Australia means that the cheap and cheerful camping option (outside the cities) can be very much a part of your travelling experience. Nothing beats being in a national park campsite under the stars, beside the open fire and within earshot of the surf, let alone in the company of several possums and a small squadron of kookaburras! Beyond resorts and national parks, other unique options include the lighthouse keepers' cottages at Green Cape, Ben Boyd (*see p162*), or vineyard stays in the Yarra (Victoria) or Barossa (South Australia) valleys (*see pp78–9 & 97*).

B&Bs, farmstays and self-catering

Rarely a budget option, most B&Bs are mid- to high-end, offering comfortable accommodation, usually en-suite, often in historic houses or on farms. Hosts are normally friendly and informative, and on farms you can join in with the day-to-day activities. Some B&Bs are actually a semi or fully self-contained cottage or cabin with breakfast supplied. As well as private houses and caravan parks, some resorts and motels provide self-contained, self-catering options. Good websites include *www.bedandbreakfast.com.au* and *www.babs.com.au*

Camping

Most national parks allow camping in designated areas. Facilities tend to be minimal, with basic toilets, fireplaces and perhaps tank water; a few have barbecues and shower blocks. Payment is often by self-registration, and barbecues often require coins. If there are fireplaces you must bring your own wood. No fires may be lit, even stoves, during a Total Fire Ban. Even if water is supposedly available, it is not guaranteed nor is it usually drinkable, so take a supply, as well as your own toilet paper. For camping details and bookings in New South Wales, contact the National Parks and Wildlife Service (*www.nationalparks.nsw.gov.au*);

in Victoria, Parks Victoria (*www.parkweb.vic.gov.au*); in Tasmania, the Tasmania Parks and Wildlife Service (*www.parks.tas.gov.au*); and in South Australia, the South Australia National Parks and Wildlife Service (*www.parks.sa.gov.au*).

Note that almost all parks charge a vehicle day-use admission charge and separate camping fees apply. Annual or multi-day passes are recommended.

Caravan and tourist parks

Almost every town has at least one caravan park with unpowered and powered sites for campers, caravans and campervans, an ablution block and usually a camp kitchen and/or barbecues. Most also provide self-contained villas and cabins. Check out **Big 4** (*Tel: 1300 738 044. www.big4.com.au*) and **Family Parks of Australia** (*Tel: 1300 855 707. www.familyparks.com.au*).

Hostels

There are many quality hostels in the main centres and all along the coast. Australia is setting the pace with the new 'flashpacker' concept, which is a modern budget hotel with all the usual hostel facilities. Most have double and twin rooms (often with en-suite) as well as single rooms and dorms. Kitchen and common-room facilities are generally good and many have free breakfast and pickup. The best hostel association is the **YHA** (*Tel: (02) 9261 1111. www.yha.org.au*).

Hotels, motels and resorts

In the state capitals there are plenty of high-end hotel options, with some like Sydney's Hyatt enjoying global recognition. In the main cities there are also many smaller boutique hotels and mid-range options. Some 'hotels' outside the major towns are traditional pubs with basic motel-style rooms with shared facilities. Motels in Australia are usually depressingly anonymous but dependably clean and comfortable. Bookings can be made through *www.accommodationgateway.com.au* or *www.lastminute.com.au*

The Hyatt Hotel, Adelaide

Food and drink

If you thought that Australian cuisine was throwing a prawn on the 'barbie', you are in for a pleasant surprise. Of course, in many a sunny backyard or at the beach, a sausage and the stalwart fish and chips still rule. But when it comes to fine dining it's a different story. With the increasingly cosmopolitan population and subsequently rich and diverse cultural influences, Modern Australian 'fusion' cuisine is rapidly developing into something dynamic, unique and world class.

Natural ingredients

Although Australia is the driest continent on earth, around its coastal fringes and along its major river basins it manages to produce a surprising abundance and variety of fruit and vegetables, from the humble head of broccoli to the exotic mango. Australia exports staple grains like wheat and produces much of its own dairy products. Beef and lamb are also home grown, as are some farmed native animals like kangaroos, emus and even crocodiles. There is also plenty of seafood, with many species of warm-water fish such as snapper. Mussels, oysters and abalone are all harvested locally. Native freshwater fish such as barramundi are in demand, as are the more conventional and farmed species like trout.

Imported Asian ingredients are commonly found in major cities because of the country's large Asian population, and include the essentials like lemon grass, chilli and Thai basil.

Markets are common, especially in rural areas where fresh locally grown fare can be bought cheaply. Organic food is still something to be enjoyed and sought after by the minority, but, like most countries, that is changing along with growing concern about genetically modified (GM) foods.

Vegetarians are generally well catered for, with some city restaurants

An enjoyable evening at the Opera House forecourt

The Mures seafood restaurant on Victoria Dock, Hobart

concentrating on just that. Although you can find some excellent European-style cafés in the cities and major towns, the distinction between cafés, bistros and restaurants is becoming somewhat blurred. Like other Western countries, fast food is also a major feature and the infamous McDonald's and Starbucks-type brands are omnipresent.

Although it all sounds like a remarkable cornucopia, the country is not immune to the impact of drought and climate change. For almost three years it has suffered its worst drought on record and the effects are beginning to be felt in supply and cost right across the board.

Drink

Australian wine needs no introduction, being a major export and having made its mark on the world scene over the last two decades. The Hunter, Barossa and Yarra vineyards are now synonymous with fine wine. In New South Wales, the Hunter Valley provides one of the best vineyard experiences in the world, with over 120 wineries, backed up by world-class accommodation, restaurants and wine-tasting tours. In Victoria, the Yarra Valley and Mornington Peninsula, and in South Australia the Barossa Valley, all enjoy an equally fine international reputation.

Compared to Europe, Australian beer and lager leave a lot to be desired, but the climate is hardly conducive to supping creamy ale at room temperature. The big brands in New South Wales are Tooheys and Castlemaine XXXX, while in Victoria, it is Victoria Bitter. As well as being available on draught in pubs, beer is available from bottleshops (or 'bottle-o's') in cases (or 'slabs') of cans ('tinnies' or 'tubes') or bottles ('stubbies'). This is by far the cheapest way of buying beer.

Entertainment

With its social history, Australia has earned a reputation as a cultural desert, but this has more to do with foreign arrogance than reality, and is certainly not the case in the cities and major towns of modern Australia. The rich cosmopolitan make-up and subsequent cultural diversity of the nation certainly offers – if not demands – an entertainment culture on a par with any other, and although (beyond the Aboriginal) it may lack some historical depth, there is no disputing the quality or diversity.

For up-to-date listings refer to the local papers. In Sydney, see The **Sydney Morning Herald** *(www.smh.com.au); in Melbourne* **The Age** *(www.theage.com.au).*

Eating out

Thanks to the tourism appeal of the east coast, restaurants are common even in smaller towns. Sydney and Melbourne are the undisputed gourmet capitals of Australia. From Sydney to Adelaide you will find the very best of Modern Australian as well as everything from French to Japanese. There is plenty of choice and, outside the high-profile city restaurants, you will find eating out generally cheaper than in Europe or the USA. Most restaurants are licensed for the consumption of alcohol. Some are Bring Your Own (BYO), in which case you provide wine or beer and there is a small corkage fee. Tipping is not mandatory, but the usual 10–15 per cent is appreciated by waiting staff.

Film and theatre

With the filming of blockbusters such as *Mad Max, Mission: Impossible, The Matrix* and, most recently, *Australia*, cinema was thriving 'down under'. However, with the global economic crisis and devalued US dollar, the film industry has suffered badly and it seems it may be some time before

The Skycity Casino, Adelaide

Australia once again becomes an attractive filming location.

Most towns have at least one venue, with some offering outdoor screenings. Prices are usually reduced on Tuesdays.

The state capitals have some excellent theatres, some of which are not only historic but of world standing. Although Australia is generally the last to see them, high-profile international shows and performances usually include Sydney and Melbourne on their tour agenda. The national talent and resident theatrical company performances are well worth investigating and annual festivals only enrich the modern repertoire.

An amusement park in Melbourne

Opera, music and dance

The Sydney Opera House is one of the best-known operatic venues in the world, and little needs to be said about opera in Australia. Classical music performances are also of the highest standard, as is contemporary dance, with one company – Bangarra – performing a unique fusion of Aboriginal and contemporary styles (*www.bangarra.com.au*).

Rock music abounds in pubs, and both national and high-profile international bands play the state capitals on a regular basis.

Pubs, clubs and casinos

The nation's many hotels, pubs and nightclubs provide much of the country's nightlife and entertainment. Rural establishments tend to espouse the traditional Aussie hotel-cum-pub aesthetic, while city establishments go for the state-of-the-art cocktail approach. As in many other countries, gimmicky pseudo-Irish pubs are common, but it is also possible to find a more authentic Euro-style, open-fire and real-ale establishment in Sydney and Melbourne.

Many establishments offer regular live music, DJs, karaoke, comedy and quiz nights, but it is perhaps gambling and the infamous 'pokies' (slot machines) that are the biggest draw, especially in rural areas. Australia is a nation of gamblers and as well as the ubiquitous slot machines, casinos are big business in Melbourne and Sydney.

Nightclubs are generally only found in the cities and are only open towards the end of the week and at weekends. They charge admission and attract the latest big-name DJs from around the world.

Shopping

With Sydney often branded alongside New York, Paris and London as one of the world capitals, it simply cannot afford to offer anything but a quality shopping experience. It certainly does not disappoint, and Melbourne is fast tapping it on the shoulder. Be it clothing or anything else, the well-known labels and brands are all in evidence and are supplemented with unique, quality Australian products like opals or Aboriginal art.

Many of Sydney's major shopping venues add to the experience, being housed in aesthetically stunning historical icons like the Queen Victoria Building, built in 1898.

Local markets are a fine place to source unique, quality Australian-made products, and you will find these in all the cities, major towns and tourist-oriented rural areas. Of course, tourist kitsch abounds and you will encounter many outlets pedalling koala backpacks and Steve Irwin (Crocodile Hunter) dolls. And as for the cork hat ... don't even go there. It may stop the flies but no Australian has ever been spotted wearing one.

Aboriginal art and craft

Almost everyone is familiar with the unique and colourful dot-style Aboriginal art. In the tourist shops these designs are as ubiquitous as cuddly koalas and printed on everything from didgeridoos to tea towels. Though beautiful, be aware that many have no

link to Aboriginal people whatsoever and so do not benefit them directly. The best thing to do is to ask the dealer directly and check the label. Beyond specialist art dealers in the city, genuine Aboriginal art and craft is more commonly available in country areas close to Aboriginal communities or from Aboriginal-owned or -operated enterprises.

In Sydney, try the **Authentic Aboriginal Art Centre** (*45 Argyle St, The Rocks. Tel: (02) 9251 4474*) or the **Boomalli Aboriginal Artists Co-operative** (*55–59 Flood St, Leichhardt. Tel: (02) 9560 2541*). The local tourist information centres can often point you in the right direction. For authentic didgeridoos look no further than **Didj Beat Didgeridoo Shop** (*Clocktower Square Mall, The Rocks. Tel: (02) 9251 4289*).

Clothing and accessories

Beyond the designer fashion labels, iconic Australian clothing generally falls into the classic 'outback' stockman image, with Akubra hats (the Australian version of the US Stetson), leather ankle boots, moleskin trousers and oilskin (Driza-Bone) rain jackets and capes the mainstay. For all these items look no further than the all-Australian company **RM Williams** (*389 George St & Shop 1–2 Chiefly Plaza, Corner Hunter St & Phillip St, Sydney. www.rmwilliams.com.au*). They have outlets or distributors in most major towns and, although pricey, the attire is of the best quality.

Australian surfwear is sought-after worldwide and is a good buy. Look for labels such as Ripcurl, Quiksilver, Mambo and Billabong.

For unique Australian fashion, try names like Scanlan and Theodore, Country Road, Collette Dinnigan and Trent Nathan, while for wearable art there is Weiss (black-and-white symbolic art often depicting native animals).

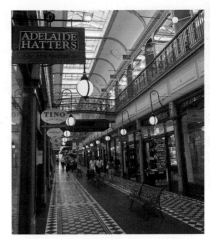

The historic Adelaide Arcade

Jewellery

With its rich geological resources, Australia has a fine range of precious gems and quality jewellery. Opals are a speciality, but pearls and diamonds are also popular. The widest range is available in the cities, with some outlets in Sydney specialising solely in opals, such as **Opal Minded** (*55 George St. Tel: (02) 9247 9885*).

Markets

In Sydney, the best markets are held every weekend in **The Rocks** (*Open: Sat & Sun*), **Paddington** (*395 Oxford St. Open: Sat*), **Glebe** (*Public School, Glebe Point Rd. Open: Sun*) and **Bondi** (*Campbell Parade. Open: Sun*). In Melbourne, the **Victoria Market** (*www.qvm.com.au*) is the big draw, while in Hobart the **Salamanca Market** (*www.salamanca.com.au*) is one of Tasmania's biggest tourist attractions.

The popular Salamanca market in Hobart

Sport and leisure

Australians love their sport, and for many it takes on an almost religious significance. Major national and international sporting events take place throughout the year and you should try to experience at least one high-profile event at a major arena such as the SCG (Sydney Cricket Ground) or MCG (Melbourne Cricket Ground). When it comes to your participation and other outdoor pursuits and activities, the great Australian climate lends itself to an array of sporting experiences.

Participatory sports and activities

Australia is one of the world's greatest adventure and activity destinations. In addition to those listed below, other well-served activities include canyoning and horse riding (Blue Mountains), cycling and mountain biking (Victoria), and golf (Sydney, and the Mornington Peninsula near Melbourne).

Specialist tour operators offer many of the best experiences, and some research before you arrive is recommended. The state, regional and local tourism websites listed throughout this guide are a good place to start.

Diving

There are many excellent dive sites all along the coast. In New South Wales, the south coast's Jervis Bay is of particular note and Tasmania has an international reputation. Visit *www.diveoz.com.au* and *www.scubaaustralia.com.au* for more information.

Fishing

Thanks to the climate and the abundance of warm saltwater species, fishing is one of Australia's favourite pastimes. Sea-fishing charters are a feature of most coastal towns, while inland some operators concentrate on freshwater species, including trout. Visit *www.fishnet.com.au* and *www.sportsfishaustralia.com.au* for details.

An abundance of fish can be found in many of the coastal towns

The AFL Grand Final, Melbourne

Four-wheel driving

Many coastal national parks in all the states offer a quality 4WD experience and are easily accessible. Outback 4WD adventures are another matter altogether and require careful planning and are best done in groups. For details, call in at a major newsagent and look at the range of Australian 4WD magazines such as *Overlander* or another popular publication, *4WD Action*.

Sea kayaking and rafting

Sea kayaking is worth considering anywhere along the coast and especially in Tasmania. White-water rafting is also a feature on the wilderness river catchments in Tasmania.

Surfing, windsurfing and kite-surfing

Sydney's many beaches are excellent, and a fine place to start. From Melbourne the Surf Coast (particularly Bells Beach) is world famous.

Lessons are readily available. Check *www.surfinfo.com.au* and *www.realsurf.com* for details.

Windsurfing and kite-surfing are also widespread, with St Kilda in Melbourne being a good place for the latter (*www.windsurfing.org*).

Spectator sports
Australian Rules Football

Also called 'Aussie rules' or just plain 'footy', to the uninitiated this winter sport is second only to cricket in being utterly baffling. Most cities and states field teams, but the true heartland is in Victoria where the Grand Final takes place every September in front of a 100,000-capacity crowd at the **MCG** (*www.mcg.org.au*).

Cricket

With almost tiring consistency, the national team ('baggy green') defeats the rest of the world at home and abroad. Cricket is a summer sport and the major venues in the Southeast are the **SCG** (*www.sydneycricketground.com.au*) and **MCG** (*www.mcg.org.au*).

Rugby

Both Rugby Union and Rugby League have a major following in Australia. The national team is known as the Wallabies and they have lifted the Rugby World Cup twice, in 1991 and again in 1999. Rugby is a winter sport, and regional and national games take place frequently in the main centres (*www.rugby.com.au*).

Australia's sporting heroes

If America's answer to royalty or celebrity is the latest Hollywood A-lister, then in Australia it is the nation's sporting heroes. It would be rude not to start with that most popular of Australian sports – cricket – and arguably the greatest sportsman of them all, Sir Donald Bradman (1908–2001). 'The Don' (as he is known) had a glittering career spanning 21 years. He represented Australia in 52 Test matches, scoring 6,996 runs, and retired with a batting average of 99.94, nearly twice that of the next nearest Test batsman. He is also noted for one innings of 452 runs for NSW at the Sydney Cricket Ground. This record still stands unchallenged as the highest-ever first-class mark compiled in Australia. On his retirement, Bradman became the first Australian player to be knighted.

Living cricketing legends, now retired, include wicketkeeper Rodney Marsh (1947–), known as 'Iron Gloves'. Dennis Lillee (1949–) was the outstanding fast bowler of his time and claimed a world-record 355 Test wickets. Much slower in pace but no less devastating was Shane Warne (1969–), widely regarded as the world's finest leg spin bowler. His 708 wickets sits in second place for the most

wickets taken in Test cricket. True to modern times, his career was plagued by scandals off the field, including a playing ban for testing positive for a prohibited substance, and his infamous 'text-message womanising'. Also known more for his antics off the field than on is Tasmanian batsman and popular personality David Boon (1960–). 'Boonie' famously drank 52 beers on a plane trip from Australia to England and ate four 72-oz steaks in one hour.

Next up, tennis and Rod Laver (1938–). He was the world's number one player in 1961, 1962, 1968 and 1969 and is one of only five players to have won all four Grand Slam singles championships – the Australian, French, US and Wimbledon – in a single year. Laver is also the only person to have done it twice, in 1962 and 1969. Evonne Goolagong Cawley (1951–) was the first Australian Aboriginal to win Wimbledon. She also won the Australian Open from 1974 to 1977 and the French Open in 1971. Other Australian tennis greats include Ken Rosewall, John Newcombe and Pat Cash.

In rugby, David Campese (1962–) was the first Australian to play 100 Test matches and is one of the world's most capped players. He was renowned for his speed and trademark 'Goosestep', holding the world record of 64 international tries. In more recent times, scrumhalf George Gregan overtook 'Campo's' record and is now the most capped Australian player.

In swimming, Shane Gould (1956–) was only 15 years old when she won three gold, one silver and a bronze at the 1972 Munich Olympic Games. She broke 11 World Records and 21 Australian Records and then retired aged 16. More recently, Ian Thorpe (1982–) won five Olympic gold medals (in 2000 and 2004), the most won by any Australian, and in 2001 he became the first person to win six gold medals in one World Championship. In total, he won 11 World Championship golds. Nicknamed the 'Thorpedo', young Ian has size 17 feet. He announced his retirement from competition in 2006.

Other sporting greats that have become household names are Greg Norman (golf), Cathy Freeman (athletics) and by no means (if ever) last, Makybe Diva, a racehorse that won the Melbourne Cup three times in a row from 2003 to 2005.

Australian Sir Donald Bradman (1908–2001), nicknamed 'The Don', still rates as the best cricketer of all time

Children

Australia is a wonderful holiday destination for children. Ask any Australian about their own childhood and they will tell you that a large part of growing up 'down under' involves being outside on the beach, in a boat, a 4WD vehicle or at a favourite campsite. Australia is full of distractions for little eyes and it is also highly aquatic, but with careful supervision there are multitudes of excellent, safe venues to keep children entertained, such as the beach, city museums and Luna Parks in Sydney and Melbourne.

Accommodation is generally no problem, with only a few of the upmarket, exclusive retreats that focus on romantic getaways unable to accept children. Many motor parks are well geared up for kids, with adventure playgrounds and child-safe swimming pools. Many tourist-based activity operations are directed at the children's market and almost every attraction or activity has family concessions or reduced rates for children. Some eateries welcome children, but you are advised to stick to eateries that are obviously child-friendly or ask before making a booking.

Beach

Little needs to be said here other than you need to keep a hat on little heads under the sun and to apply copious amounts of sunblock. Also counsel your charges on the need to 'swim between the flags' and recognise what a lifeguard looks like.

You will generally find most public beaches are patrolled from December to March, with some city beaches having a year-round presence. In

An annual summer surfing contest

THE LYREBIRD

Australia is home to many remarkable birds with many amazing attributes, but when it comes to acoustics the Lyrebird makes an opera singer look amateur.

There are two species: the Superb Lyrebird, found in the rainforests of New South Wales, Victoria and Tasmania, and Albert's Lyrebird, only found in southern Queensland. They are called Lyrebirds because of their decorative 'lyrate' (in the shape of a lyre) tail feathers.

However, it is their song for which they are most well known. This is a mix of their own sounds and others that they have heard and copied. In fact, the lyrebird has the most developed syrinx of any bird and arguably the most complex repertoire of any species. Lyrebirds are capable of imitating almost any sound in nature or created by humans, including machinery and musical instruments. Given the sheer number of noises people are capable of making, there is plenty of scope. Well-known renditions have included saws, dogs, fire alarms, explosions, camera shutters and mobile phone ring-tones.

Lyrebirds are generally shy in the wild but adapt well to captivity. Many zoos and wildlife sanctuaries host them, and the Healesville Sanctuary near Melbourne is especially recommended (see p81).

Sydney, Bondi, Manly, Balmoral and Coogee beaches are all good safe options, with many having purpose-built pools. Near Melbourne don't miss the Port Phillip Bay beaches along the Mornington Peninsula.

Wildlife

Despite its misinformed reputation for baby-snatching dingoes, man-eating sharks, venomous snakes and spiders, wildlife is a fundamental component of the Australian holiday experience for both young and old. If you are at all concerned about the rumoured threat of Australia's native wildlife, take a trip to Sydney's Taronga Zoo (see p39), Healesville Sanctuary near Melbourne (see p81), or indeed any of the numerous wildlife parks throughout the Southeast. Whether captive or not, Australia's abundant wildlife offers one of the greatest natural history education platforms for children on the planet and encounters with wildlife can become any foreign child's fondest memory. Australian children have a healthy respect and love for the outdoors and wildlife borne through exposure and good education. As such, mixing with Australian kids is an ideal way for yours to learn.

Sun savvy

Essentials

Arriving and departing
By air

The vast majority of travellers arrive by air into Sydney or Melbourne. The principal international airports for southeast Australia are Sydney, Melbourne and Adelaide (usually all available if you are travelling on a Round the World (RTW) ticket).

There are many international carriers, with **Qantas** (Australia's main airline; *www.qantas.com.au*), **Air New Zealand** (*www.airnewzealand.com*) and **Emirates** (*www.emirates.com*) being the main companies.

If you are travelling from Europe or North America, an expensive long-haul flight is unavoidable, but from Europe this can be treated as an opportunity for a brief stopover either in the USA (Los Angeles or San Francisco), the Middle East (Dubai), or Asia (Singapore, Bangkok or Kuala Lumpur). Most airlines can help you to offset your carbon footprint.

Fares are high during December and January unless booked well in advance. Mid-year tends to see the cheapest fares. The Internet is the best place to secure cheap flights. If arriving from or via the USA, you will be allowed two pieces of hold luggage up to a total of 75kg (165lb), plus carry-on per person, while all other routes only allow one piece per person at 20kg (44lb) plus carry-on.

Sydney's **Kingsford Smith Airport** is 9km (5¹/₂ miles) south of the city centre (*www.sydneyairport.com*). The fastest and most convenient way into town is to use the Airport Link rail service every 10–15 minutes. Taxis available outside the terminal take 30 minutes. Various independent or courtesy shuttles also operate door to door. Melbourne's **Tullamarine Airport** is 25km (15¹/₂ miles) from the Central Business District and is well served by public transport (*www.melbourneairport.com.au*).

By sea

Cruise liners regularly visit Australia on world, Pacific or New Zealand and Australia tours. The main ports of call are Sydney, Melbourne and Hobart. The main operators are **Princess Cruises** (*www.princess.com*) and **P&O** (*www.pocruises.com*). Fly-cruise packages are also an option.

Customs

The limits for duty-free goods brought into the country include 2.25 litres of alcohol per person (18 years or over)

Hobart's Salamanca Place at night

and 250 cigarettes or 250g of cigars or tobacco. There are various import restrictions primarily involving live plants and animals, plant and animal materials (including wood) and foodstuffs. Declare any such items if you are unsure (*www.customs.gov.au*).

Electricity

The current in Australia is 240/250V AC. Plugs have two- or three-blade pins. To use appliances from the UK or USA you will need an adaptor.

Internet

Fast connection is readily available in Internet outlets, cafés, libraries and most accommodation, and in all major cities and towns. Rural areas can be a problem. Wireless capability is improving but is not as widespread as in Europe or the USA.

Media

The only nationwide daily is *The Australian* (*Mon–Fri with weekend edition. www.theaustralian.news.com.au*). In Sydney and New South Wales, the main newspaper is *The Sydney Morning Herald* (*Mon–Fri with weekend edition. www.smh.com.au*) and in Melbourne, it is the *Herald Sun* (*Mon–Sat with Sun edition*). In Hobart, it is the *Mercury* (*Mon–Sat with Sun edition. www.news.com.au/mercury*) and in Adelaide *The Adelaide Advertiser* (*Mon–Sat*) and *Sunday Mail* (*www.news.com.au/adelaidenow*).

The Australian Geographic magazine (*www.australiangeographic.com.au*) is recommended.

The main TV channels are the highly commercial, mainstream channels of 7, 9 and 10, with less sensationalist material on ABC (*www.abc.net.au*) and SBS (*www.sbs.com.au*). As in most countries, the subscription to Foxtel (Sky) TV is popular, especially for sports coverage.

Money

The Australian dollar ($ or AU$ to distinguish it from other dollar currencies) is divided into 100 cents (c). Coins come in denominations of 5c, 10c, 20c, 50c, $1 and $2. Banknotes come in denominations of $5, $10, $20, $50 and $100.

Most operators and outlets accept all the major credit cards. You can withdraw cash from ATMs with a cash card or credit card issued by most international banks, and they can also be used at banks, post offices and bureaux de change.

Traveller's cheques are accepted for exchange in banks, large hotels, post offices and large gift shops. The four major banks, Westpac, Commonwealth, NAB and ANZ, are usually the best places to change money and traveller's cheques as they offer the most competitive rates and branches are commonplace. Bureaux de change are located at all major airports and in the city centres.

Opening hours

Opening hours are usually as follows:
Banks Mon–Fri 9.30am–4 or 5pm
Offices Mon–Fri 8.30am–5pm
Shops Mon–Fri 9am–5.30pm, Sat
9am–5pm, Sun 11am–5pm.

However, many city shops remain open later. Convenience stores and supermarkets are generally open seven days a week until mid-evening or later.

Passports and visas

All travellers to Australia, except New Zealand citizens, must have a valid visa. These need to be arranged prior to travel (allow two months) and cannot be organised at Australian airports. Tourist visas are free and are available from your local Australian Embassy or High Commission or, in some countries, in electronic format (an Electronic Travel Authority or ETA) from the embassy websites, and from selected travel agents and airlines. Passport holders from most European countries, the USA and Canada are eligible to apply for an ETA. Tourist visas allow visits of up to three months within the year after the visa is issued. If you are visiting for longer than three months, or are not eligible for an ETA, you may be able to apply for a

The Richmond Arms, Tasmania

visitor or work visa. For details, visit
www.eta.immi.gov.au

Pharmacies

Pharmacies are widely available in most centres with at least one open late or 24 hours. Addresses and map locations can be found in the Yellow Pages
(*www.yellowpages.com.au*).

Post

Australia Post has outlets in all the main centres. Opening hours follow standard business hours with the exception of some major outlets that also open on Saturday mornings. Post boxes are red. For details, see *www.auspost.com.au*

Public holidays

1 January – New Year's Day
26 January – Australia Day
Second Monday in March – Labor Day (VIC and TAS)
March/April (variable) – Good Friday and Easter Monday
25 April – ANZAC Day
Second Monday in June – Queen's Birthday
First Monday in October – Labor Day (NSW and SA)
First Tuesday in November – Melbourne Cup Day (Metropolitan Melbourne only)
25 and 26 December – Christmas and Boxing Day

Smoking

About 17 per cent of Australians are smokers. Smoking is now illegal in pubs, restaurants, cafés and most public buildings (including airports). It is also prohibited on all forms of public transport (including taxis). Many establishments do, however, accommodate smokers outdoors.

Tax

Almost all goods in Australia are subject to a Goods and Services Tax (GST) of 10 per cent. Certain shops can deduct the GST if you show a valid departure ticket. For details, see *www.customs.gov.au*

Telephones

Most public payphones are operated by Telstra (*www.telstra.com.au*). Some take phonecards, available from newsagents and post offices, and credit cards.

Telephoning southeast Australia from abroad
Dial the international prefix followed by *61*, then the state phone code minus the first *0*, then the eight-digit number.
Note: There are no area phone codes in Australia, just state codes:
Australian Capital Territory/New South Wales *02*
South Australia *08*
Victoria/Tasmania *03*

Telephoning abroad from Australia
Dial *0011* followed by the country code:
New Zealand *64*
South Africa *27*
UK *44*
USA and Canada *1*

Directory enquiries *1223*
International directory enquiries *1225*

There are many mobile phone companies, including Telstra, Vodafone and Optus. The cheapest way of calling overseas is to use an international pre-paid phonecard (such as Yabba or E-Phone) available from city post offices and newsagents.

Time

Australia covers three time zones, with Victoria, Tasmania and New South Wales using Eastern Standard Time (GMT plus ten hours). Daylight saving applies from October to March, when clocks go forward one hour. South Australia (Adelaide) is 30 minutes behind Victoria, New South Wales and Tasmania.

Toilets

Public toilets are widely available, free and generally of a good standard. At the beach a toilet and shower block is often attached to the many publicly accessible surf lifesaving clubs.

Travellers with disabilities

Facilities for travellers with disabilities are generally good, especially in the main centres. Many accommodation, transport and activity operators provide facilities, and most major sights and attractions and even parks have good access. The **Access Foundation** can provide details (*Tel: 1300 797 025. www.accessibility.com.au*). In Sydney, the free leaflet 'CBD Access Map Sydney' is available from visitor information centres.

Language

English is the main language, but many words and sayings are specific to the country. Australian English is sometimes referred to as 'Strine'. Of course some words like 'mate' are known the world over, but you must beware of stereotypes.

Common words and phrases

arvo	afternoon
bananabender	someone from Queensland
beauty ('bewdy')	excellent, fantastic (often preceded by 'you')
billy	kettle (non-electric)
bludger	layabout, lazy person
bottleshop ('bottle-o')	off-licence or liquor outlet
chook	chicken
chunder	vomit
dag or **daggy**	dirty wool around sheep's backend, also 'uncool'
doona	duvet
dunny	toilet
esky	portable cool box
fair dinkum	fair, the truth
grommet	young surfer
hard yakka	hard work
jug	kettle (electric)
larrikin	mischievous person
lay-by	keep aside until paid for
mullet	hairstyle (especially 1980s)
no worries	not a problem, no bother
op-shop	second-hand shop
park	parking space
pokies	gambling slot machines
rego	car registration
ripper	excellent (often preceded by 'you')
score	to secure something often for free, or a date with a girl
she'll be right	everything will be OK
slab	crate of beer, usually 24 bottles or cans
smoko	work break
snag	sausage
stubbie	can of beer
swag	canvas sleeping bag and mattress in one
thongs	flip-flops
tinnie	can of beer or a small aluminium boat
tucker	food
ute	utility vehicle
yabby	edible freshwater crustacean similar to lobster

Emergencies

Healthcare

Australia has a national, government-funded healthcare scheme called Medicare, together with a private healthcare network. Public hospitals are part of Medicare and most doctors are registered so that their services can be funded or subsidised by the scheme. Australia has reciprocal arrangements with a handful of countries, which allow citizens of those countries to receive free 'immediately necessary medical treatment' under the Medicare scheme, but this does not include travel by ambulance. Check with your travel agent or national health scheme whether you qualify for Medicare and what documents you will require in Australia to claim. All visitors are, however, strongly advised to take out medical insurance for the duration of their visit.

No vaccinations are required for entry into Australia but you are advised to get a tetanus booster. The Traveller's Medical and Vaccination Centre (TMVC) operates several clinics around the country, including in Sydney (*Level 7, 428 George St. Tel: (02) 9221 7133. www.tmvc.com.au*). Medical facilities in individual towns and cities are listed in the telephone directories. See also *www.health.gov.au*

Health risks

When it comes to personal safety, Australia certainly has its dangers, but with a little common sense and basic precautions they are relatively easy to minimise. The sun is a major factor. UV (ultraviolet) levels can soar in Australia, with safe exposure limits as low as three minutes, so wear a hat and shades and use sunblock. Also be careful of dehydration and drink plenty of fluids.

With road travel, beware of fatigue as well as large native or stock animals (especially kangaroos and wombats in rural areas at dawn or dusk). Hitchhiking is not recommended.

Protect yourself from the sun

On the beach always swim between the patrolled flags and be aware of hidden dangers like rips – strong offshore undertows. Avoid swimming alone, and keep swimming partners in sight. While snorkelling or diving, do not touch either creatures or coral. In summer, members of Surf Life Saving Australia patrol many public beaches and they are always the best source for advice and assistance (*www.slsa.asn.au*).

Australia has a terrible reputation when it comes to sharks and venomous wildlife. Although there are some real dangers, the threats are over-exaggerated and with a little common sense your encounters with wildlife will be nothing but pleasant. Shark attacks do occur, but are extremely rare. Snakes and spiders will generally get out of your way unless harassed, and by avoiding swimming in the ocean north of Townsville from November to March you will avoid the well-publicised risk of marine stingers (potentially fatal small jellyfish) or other venomous sea creatures.

Crime

Australia has average crime rates and tourists are often targeted in both urban and rural areas. The common-sense approach applies to personal safety and possessions. Travel insurance is recommended with premium add-ons that include specific items like cameras or laptops. Check the small print!

Currents can be dangerous, so never swim alone

Embassies and consulates

Canada
Level 5, 111 Harrington St, Sydney. Tel: (02) 9364 3000. www.canadaonline.about.com

Germany
13 Trelawney St, Woollahra, Sydney. Tel: (02) 9328 7733. www.germanembassy.org.au

New Zealand
Level 10, 55 Hunter St, Sydney. Tel: (02) 8256 2000. www.nzembassy.com

South Africa
Rhodes Place, State Circle, Yarralumla, Canberra, ACT. Tel: (02) 6273 2424. www.sahc.org.au

UK
Level 16, The Gateway, 1 Macquarie Pl, Sydney. Tel: (02) 9247 7521. www.ukinaustralia.fco.gov.uk

USA
19–29 Martin Pl, Sydney. Tel: (02) 9373 9200. http://sydney.usconsulate.gov

Directory

Accommodation price guide

Prices of accommodation are based on a double room (or a powered site at a motor park) per night for two people sharing in the high season (with breakfast where applicable).

★	Up to AU$55
★★	AU$55–AU$175
★★★	AU$175–AU$250
★★★★	Over AU$250

Eating out price guide

Prices are based on an average three-course meal for one, without drinks.

★	Up to AU$15
★★	AU$15–AU$25
★★★	AU$25–AU$30
★★★★	Over AU$30

SYDNEY

ACCOMMODATION

Lord Nelson Pub and Hotel ★★
A fine historic hotel at the edge of The Rocks, which has some pleasant and affordable en-suites above the pub. The added attractions are the home-brewed beer and general ambience. The pub closes fairly early at night, so noise is generally not a problem.
Corner of Kent & Argyle Sts, The Rocks.
Tel: (02) 9251 4044.
www.lordnelson.com.au

Glenferrie Lodge ★★–★★★
Large 70-room Victorian mansion in a quiet location, yet only a short walk from Kirribilli, ferry terminals and the Harbour Bridge. There is a full range of shared, single, twin or double rooms, some with a balcony and city view. Cheap quality dinners and breakfast buffets.
12A Carabella St.
Tel: (02) 9955 1685.
www.glenferrielodge.com.au

Trickett's Luxury B&B ★★★
A restored Victorian mansion in Glebe, 'the village within the city'. Spacious, nicely appointed en-suites with antiques and Persian rugs throughout. Off-street parking and generous continental breakfast.
270 Glebe Point Rd.
Tel: (02) 9552 1141.
www.tricketts.com.au

Park Hyatt ★★★★
Hugely popular thanks to its waterside location overlooking the Sydney Opera House. Faultless in presentation, with all mod cons. A fine restaurant on the ground floor proves the ideal spot from which to watch the activity on the harbour.
7 Hickson Rd.
Tel: (02) 9241 1234. www.sydney.park.hyatt.com

EATING OUT

Harry's Café de Wheels ★
Dispensing famously yummy pies with pea toppings and gravy at

all hours of the night and day, Harry's is something of a Sydney institution. One is surely never enough.
Corner Cowper Wharf Rd & Brougham St, Woolloomooloo.
Tel: (02) 9211 2506.
Open: 24 hours.

Botanic Gardens Restaurant ★–★★
A fine escape from the city, with the added attraction of a nearby colony of flying foxes (fruit bats). Utterly clean, enchanting and mesmerising.
Mrs Macquaries Rd, City.
Tel: (02) 9241 2419.
Open: Mon–Fri noon–3pm, Sat & Sun 9.30am–3pm.

Doyle's on the Beach ★★★–★★★★
Arguably Sydney's best-known seafood beachside restaurant in the eastern suburb of Watson's Bay. The general atmosphere and views across the harbour and city skyline are hard to beat. If you can, book a balcony seat. Sunday afternoons are especially popular

and you can combine the trip with a walk around the heads. Book ahead.
11 Marine Parade.
Tel: (02) 9337 2007.
www.doyles.com.au.
Open: noon–3pm & 6–9pm.

Forty-one Restaurant ★★★★
Even without the commanding views across the Botanic Gardens and harbour, this long-established favourite is deserving of an international reputation for fine dining. Intimate yet relaxed. Bookings essential.
Chifley Tower, 2 Chifley Square, City.
Tel: (02) 9221 2500.
www.forty-one.com.au.
Open: lunch Tue–Fri from noon, dinner Mon–Sat from 6pm.

ENTERTAINMENT
Australian Heritage Hotel
Along with the Lord Nelson (*see Accommodation listing p159*), this is a Sydney classic with a mixed clientele and good

atmosphere right in the heart of The Rocks.
100 Cumberland St, The Rocks.
Tel: (02) 9247 2229.
www.australian heritagehotel.com.
Open: 11am–late.

Bangarra
An excellent contemporary Aboriginal dance group.
Wharf 4, Walsh Bay.
Tel: (02) 9251 5333.
www.bangarra.com.au

Hayden Orpheum Cinema
Fully restored Art Deco cinema offering a fine alternative to the more modern city cinemas.
380 Military Rd, Cremorne.
Tel: (02) 9908 4344.
www.orpheum.com.au

Home Nightclub
Dubbed a 'super club' and spread over four levels, this is one of the country's largest. Here, you can even 'kinkidisco' – the mind boggles.
Cockle Bay Wharf, Darling Harbour.
Tel: (02) 9266 0600.
www.homesydney.com.
Open: 10pm–6am.
Admission charge.

Opera House and Concourse

The Opera House has five performance venues offering everything from Billy Connolly to Andrea Bocelli. There are also several bars with open-air tables in the shadow of the great Opera House and overlooking Circular Quay and the Harbour Bridge. For casual drinks there is arguably no place more quintessentially Sydney than this, but beware, the drinks are heavily overpriced and it does get very busy.
Circular Quay East.
Box office.
Tel: (02) 9250 7777.
www.soh.nsw.gov.au

Wharf Theatre

Home of the world-renowned Sydney Theatre Company.
Opposite Pier 6/7,
22 Hickson Rd, The Rocks.
Tel: (02) 9250 1999.
www.sydneytheatre.org.au

Bonza Bike Tours

Attack the sights with pedal power. There are guided or self-guided options from two hours

to half a day. Independent hire is also available.
Tel: (02) 9331 1127.
www.bonzabiketours.com

Bridge Climb

The famous ascent of the 134m (440ft) Harbour Bridge span. The three-hour climb can be done day or night and in most weather conditions. Stunning views guaranteed.
3 Cumberland St,
The Rocks.
Tel: (02) 8274 7777.
www.bridgeclimb.com

Manly Surf School

Good-value daily classes from 11am to 1pm.
North Steyne Surf Club,
Manly Beach.
Tel: (02) 9977 6977.
www.manlysurfschool.com

Sydney by Sail

Based at the National Maritime Museum and offering social day trips and introductory lessons.
National Maritime Museum, Darling Harbour.
Tel: (02) 9280 1110.
www.sydneybysail.com

Sydney Harbour Kayaks

Explore the inner harbour inlets and bays.

Guided or self-guided trips available.
Spit Bridge, Mosman.
Tel: (02) 9960 4389.
www.sydneyharbour kayaks.com.au

SOUTHEAST COAST: SYDNEY TO MELBOURNE
Bateman's Bay
ACCOMMODATION
Bateman's Bay Beach Resort ★–★★

Quality beachside resort offering the full range of accommodation, from spacious cabins to tent sites. Good facilities including camp kitchen, pool, shop and free wireless Internet.
51 Beach Rd.
Tel: (02) 4472 4541.
www.beachresort.com.au

EATING OUT
On The Pier ★★★

Fine dining, with locally caught seafood the speciality. Ask for a seat overlooking the river. Vegetarian options are available.
Old Punt Rd.
Tel: (02) 4472 6405.
www.onthepier.com.au.
Open: noon–2.30pm &
6–8.30pm.

SPORT AND LEISURE

Bay and Beyond Sea Kayak Tours
38 Lakeside Dr,
South Durras.
Tel: (02) 4478 7777.
www.
bayandbeyond.com.au

Eden and Ben Boyd National Park

ACCOMMODATION AND EATING OUT

Green Cape Lighthouse Keepers' Cottages ★★–★★★
A true coastal getaway. Two fully self-contained assistant keepers' cottages accommodating up to six people.
Lighthouse Rd,
Ben Boyd National Park.
Tel: (02) 6495 5000.
www.lighthouse.net.au &
www.npws.nsw.gov.au

Crown and Anchor B&B ★★★
Former hotel originally built in 1845 with lots of character. Classy en-suite rooms with claw-foot baths, open fires and great views across Twofold Bay.
239 Imlay St, Eden.
Tel: (02) 6496 1017.
www.crownandanchor
eden.com.au

Seahorse Inn ★★★
Historic, luxury boutique hotel named after the steamship on which Ben Boyd arrived in Australia. Built in the 1840s and full of character, it offers tidy, spacious en-suites and a good bar and restaurant.
Just off the Princes Hwy,
8km (5 miles) south
of Eden.
Tel: (02) 6496 1361.
www.seahorseinn.com.au.
Open: lunch noon–2pm,
dinner Mon–Sat 6–8pm.

Jervis Bay

ACCOMMODATION AND EATING OUT

Paperbark Camp ★★★★
Luxury eco-oriented en-suite tent units in a tranquil bush setting. There is an outdoor campfire, good on-site restaurant (open to non-guests), tours and activities (book ahead).
605 Woollamia Rd.
Tel: (02) 4441 6066.
www.paperbarkcamp.
com.au. Open: dinner
daily from 6pm.
Closed: Jul & Aug.

SPORT AND LEISURE

Dive Jervis Bay
Boat dives, snorkelling and equipment hire for some of the New South Wales south coast's best sites.
64 Owen St, Huskisson.
Tel: (02) 4441 5255.
www.
divejervisbay.com.au

Dolphin Watch Jervis Bay
Two- to three-hour cruises sighting dolphins year-round, and both dolphins and whales June to November. There is also a twilight BBQ Cruise.
50 Owen St,
Huskisson.
Tel: (02) 4441 6311.
www.
dolphinwatch.com.au

Narooma and Tilba

ACCOMMODATION

Dromedary Hotel ★★
Historic pub with character located right in the heart of the village. Traditional basic B&B rooms and good-value counter meals.
Bate St, Central Tilba.
Tel: (02) 4473 7223.

Ecotel ★★

As the name suggests, an eco-friendly motel-style establishment with the owners making every effort to combine clean, value accommodation with ecological benefits.
44 Princes Hwy.
Tel: (02) 4476 2217.
www.ecotel.com.au

Priory at Bingie ★★

Quality architecture, landscape and art merge in this modern, stylish and good-value B&B. Well-presented double rooms, plenty of peace and quiet and great ocean views. In-house gallery.
Priory Lane,
Bingie (26km/16 miles
north of Narooma).
Tel: (02) 4473 8881.
www.bingie.com

EATING OUT

Quarterdeck Marina ★★

Café-style fare amid a good atmosphere with fine views across the marina from the deck.
13 Riverside Dr.
Tel: (02) 4476 2723.
Open: 8am onwards.

Victorian border to Lakes Entrance

ACCOMMODATION

Bellbrae ★★

Self-contained log cabins in a peaceful forest setting.
4km (2¹/₂ miles) north
of Lakes Entrance on
Ostlers Rd.
Tel: (03) 5155 2319.
www.lakes-entrance.com

Point Hicks Lighthouse Keepers' Cottages ★★–★★★

At a remote location (*50 mins from the Princes Hwy*) deep within the Croajingolong National Park, with verandas overlooking the sea and three bedrooms sleeping six. Not cheap, but unique and heavily booked at peak times. There is also a budget bungalow with basic facilities. Be sure to book well in advance at this popular location.
Croajingolong National
Park.
Tel: (03) 5158 4268.
www.pointhicks.com.au

Déjà Vu ★★★

Modern B&B set in 3ha (7 acres) of wild lakeside country.

Suites with private lake-view balconies and first-class service. There are a couple of self-contained properties fronting the lake. Book well in advance.
North of Lakes Entrance
overlooking the lake
on Clara St.
Tel: (03) 5155 4330.
www.dejavu.com.au

EATING OUT

Ferryman's Seafood Café ★★–★★★

Former ferry now one of the region's best options for fine dining.
Middle Boat Harbour,
The Esplanade.
Tel: (03) 5155 3000.
www.ferrymans.com.au.
Open: lunch noon–3pm,
dinner from 6pm.

CANBERRA
City centre

ACCOMMODATION

Canberra City YHA ★–★★

Pitched between a modern backpackers' and budget hotel. Close to the city centre with plenty of rooms from dorms to en-suite doubles.

Well facilitated with kitchen, bar, pool and spa.
7 Akuna St, City Centre. Tel: (02) 6248 9155. www.yha.com.au
Hotel Kurrajong ★★★
One of the capital's best boutique hotels, near the lively suburbs of Manuka and Kingston. A fine range of rooms with classy, modern décor and good dinner, bed and breakfast packages.
*8 National Circuit, Barton.
Tel: (02) 6234 4444.
www.hotelkurrajong. com.au*
Hyatt Hotel ★★★–★★★★
Arguably the most high-profile of Canberra's hotels, this heritage-listed building (built in 1924) is surrounded by landscaped gardens and has beautifully appointed rooms and suites. The Art Deco-influenced foyer is particularly memorable.
*Commonwealth Ave, Yarralumla.
Tel: (02) 6270 1234.
www. canberra.park.hyatt.com*

EATING OUT
Gus's Café ★★
One of the best city-centre cafés, especially good for breakfast.
*Shop 8, Garema Arcade, Bunda St.
Tel: (02) 6248 8118.
Open: Mon–Fri 7.30am–10.30pm, Sat & Sun 7.30am–11.59pm.*
My Café ★★
Long-established favourite, with a laid-back atmosphere and al-fresco street dining. It is especially good for Sunday brunch and coffee.
Shop 1, Manuka Arcade, Manuka. Tel: (02) 6295 6632. Open: daily 8am until late.
Boat House by the Lake ★★★
A firm favourite set on the banks of Lake Burley Griffin. Modern Australian cuisine and a fine lunch venue.
*Grevillea Park, Menindee Dr, Barton.
Tel: (02) 6273 5500.
Open: lunch Mon–Fri noon–2pm, dinner Mon–Sat 6.30–9pm.*
The Chairman and Yip ★★★
Large, centrally located Asian restaurant, popular for its good-value Chinese cuisine with an Aussie edge.
*108 Bunda St, Civic.
Tel: (02) 6248 7109. www. thechairmanandyip.com.
Open: lunch Tue–Fri noon–2.30pm, dinner Mon–Sat 6–10.30pm.*

ENTERTAINMENT
Canberra Theatre Centre
The theatre centre hosts several live entertainment venues under one roof and a dynamic, eclectic range of shows from contemporary dance to Bollywood.
*Civic Square.
Tel: (02) 6275 2700.
www. canberratheatre.org.au*
Casino Canberra
Not to be outdone by the other state capitals, Canberra has a casino. There is lots of live entertainment to supplement the gaming with dinner and show packages.
*21 Binara St.
Tel: (02) 6257 7074.
www. casinocanberra.com.au.
Open: noon–6am.*

Greater Union Cinema

Civic Greater Union is the most centrally placed cinema, offering the best mainstream films. Tuesday night is discount night.
Franklin St, Manuka.
Tel: (02) 6247 5522.
www.greaterunion.com.au

Wig and Pen

Centrally located pub with plenty of character. Especially good on a Friday evening.
Alinga St, City Centre.
Tel: (02) 6248 0171.
www.wigandpen.com.au.
Open: daily lunch & dinner.

SPORT AND LEISURE

Balloon Aloft

Dawn balloon flights over the city.
Tel: (02) 6285 1540.
www.balloonaloft.com.au

Dawn Drifters

Another company offering dawn balloon flights over the city.
Tel: (02) 6285 4450.
www.dawndrifters.com.au

Real Fun

Kayak trips on Lake Burley Griffin. The company also offers abseiling, canyoning, mountain biking and rafting around the region.
Tel: (02) 6228 1264.
www.realfun.com.au

Southern Cross Cruises

Daily cruise schedules on Lake Burley Griffin with stops at the National Museum, Questacon or Commonwealth Park. Lunch and dinner cruises are also available.
Tel: (02) 6273 1784.
Departs (10am & 3pm) from Regatta Point, near the National Capital Exhibition Building on Regatta Place.

Snowy Mountains

ACCOMMODATION

Kosciuszko Mountain Retreat ★–★★

This retreat is in a great bush setting with lots of wildlife and local walks.
Sawpit Creek, 14km (9 miles) east of Jindabyne, up the Perisher Valley.
Tel: (02) 6456 2224.
www.kositreat.com.au

Pender Lea Chalets ★★–★★★

A range of options on offer from a mobile home, a rustic (renovated) hut and a bedsitter, through to fully self-contained luxury cottages and chalets, all set in its own 1,133ha (2,800-acre) property. Horse riding is an added attraction.
Alpine Way, 11km (7 miles) from Jindabyne.
Tel: (02) 6456 2088.
www.penderlea.com.au

Novotel Lake Crackenback Resort ★★★★

Fully equipped luxury lakeside resort with modern self-contained apartments overlooking the lake. There is a good restaurant, pool, sauna and sports facilities.
Close to the 'Skitube' transport to ski fields.
Alpine Way 16km (10 miles) from Jindabyne.
Tel: (02) 6451 3000. www. novotellakecrackenback. com.au

EATING OUT

Banjo Paterson Inn ★★

Atmospheric pub with good-value bar meals and live entertainment. Also offers good accommodation handy for town.

At the western end of Jindabyne on Kosciuszko Rd. Tel: (02) 6456 2372. www.banjopatersoninn. com.au. Open: daily lunch & dinner.

SPORT AND LEISURE
The National Parks Wildlife Service Visitor Centre (Hiking)
Provides hiking and walks information.
Jindabyne, Kosciuszko Rd. Tel: (02) 6450 5600. www. nationalparks.nsw.gov.au
Perisher Blue (Skiing)
Provides detailed skiing information.
Tel: 1300 655 822. www.perisherblue.com.au
Thredbo Visitors Information Centre (Skiing)
6 Friday Dr, Thredbo, just opposite the river and bridges to the ski fields. Tel: (02) 6459 4294/ 1800 020 589. www.thredbo.com.au

MELBOURNE AND CENTRAL VICTORIA
Melbourne
ACCOMMODATION
Melbourne Central YHA ★–★★
One of YHA Australia's biggest and newest

hostels. Renovated, 208-bed, five-storey, heritage-listed building, ideally located near the corner of Flinders and Spencer Streets in the Central Business District. Full range of rooms and facilities with the usual reliable standards.
562 Flinders St. Tel: (03) 9621 2523. www.yha.com.au
Jasper Hotel ★★–★★★
Newly renovated contemporary hotel located on the fringe of the Central Business District. Good-value double, twin and two-bedroom suites. Pool, cable TV and wireless Internet. Breakfast available and discounted parking nearby.
489 Elizabeth St. Tel: (03) 8327 2777. www.jasperhotel.com.au
Villa Donati ★★★
Excellent boutique hotel located 2.5km (1½ miles) from the city centre. Chic, classy rooms with a mix of European and Asian furnishings. Café-style breakfast. On-street parking.

377 Church St. Tel: (03) 9428 8104. www.villadonati.com
Hotel Windsor ★★★★
Melbourne's grandest hotel and one of its most opulent. Built in 1883 and set overlooking Parliament House and Treasury Gardens, it exudes both character and class. And the rooms? Well, here you even have a pillow menu! The restaurant and cocktail bar (One Eleven Spring Street) is also famous for its English-style afternoon teas.
111 Spring St. Tel: (03) 9633 6000. www.thewindsor.com.au

EATING OUT
Pellegrinis ★–★★
Melbourne's original Italian espresso bar opened in 1954 and it hasn't really changed much. Excellent coffee (of course) and cheap pasta dishes.
66 Bourke St. Tel: (03) 9662 1885. Open: Mon–Sat 8am–11.30pm, Sun noon–8pm.
Topolinos ★–★★
If you get peckish in St Kilda and have

avoided the cake shops, this is a fine choice. Well established and always busy, it is perhaps most notable for its excellent cheap pizza and pasta.
87 Fitzroy St, St Kilda. Tel: (03) 9534 4856. Open: Thur–Sun noon–late, Mon–Wed 4pm–late.

Cutler and Co
★★★–★★★★
New and highly regarded restaurant/bar owned by celebrity chef Andrew McConnell. His former restaurant, Three, One, Two in Carlton, was his prelude to Cutler and Co and his success continues unabated. Set in a former metalwork factory, the architecture successfully marries both the old and new creating a chic atmosphere that is both informal and relaxed. Brilliantly imaginative and inventive cuisine that offers one of the best dining experiences in Australia – provided you can get a booking!
55–57 Gertrude St, Fitzroy. Tel: (03) 9419 4888. www.cutlerandco.com.au. Restaurant open: Tue–Sun for dinner from 6pm; Fri

& Sat for lunch from noon. Bar open: Tue–Sun 4pm–midnight.

Rockpool Bar and Grill ★★★★
One of Melbourne's many award winners but well in the top five. Home of lauded chef Neil Perry, who is renowned for 'turning great produce into something memorable'. Steak is a house speciality.
Crown Complex, Southbank Tel: (03) 8648 1900. www.rockpoolmelbourne. com. Open: lunch Sun–Fri noon–3pm, dinner daily from 6pm.

ENTERTAINMENT
Cinema
Village cinemas are located at 206 Bourke St (*Tel: (03) 9667 6565*), the Crown Complex, Southgate (*Tel: (03) 9278 6666*), and The Jam Factory, 500 Chapel St, Prahan (*Tel: 1300 555 400*). *www.villagecinemas.com.au*

Comedy Club
First established in 1975 and considered *the* place for an organised laugh.

Hosts local, national and international talent.
188 Collins St. Tel: (03) 9650 6668. www.thecomedyclub.com.au

Crown Casino
With a gaming floor stretching over 1km (^{2}/$_3$ mile), this is one of the Southern Hemisphere's largest casinos. It's not all gambling, with plenty of live entertainment, big-screen TVs, restaurants and even high-stakes bingo.
Southbank. Tel: (03) 9292 8888. www.crowncasino.com.au

Dizzy's Jazz Club
Regularly hosts live jazz. Check the playlist on *www.dizzys.com.au*.
381 Burnley St, Richmond. Tel: (03) 9428 1233. Open: Tue–Thur from 7pm, Fri & Sat from 5.30pm.

Hairy Canary
A trendy Central Business District bar and café that maintains its popularity with fickle Melbournian pub-goers. Rocks well into the early hours.
212 Little Collins St. Tel: (03) 9654 2471.

*Open: Mon–Fri
7.30am–3am, Sat
9am–3am, Sun
10am–1am.*

The Laundry
One of the city's best
nightclubs hosting
world-renowned DJs.
*50 Johnston St, Fitzroy.
Tel: (03) 9419 7111.
Open: 3pm–3am.*

SPORT AND LEISURE
Go Wild Ballooning
Melbourne has a well-
established reputation
for early morning
scenic flights – weather
permitting. Champagne
breakfast flights available
for one hour.
*Tel: (03) 9739 0772.
www.gowildballooning.
com.au*
**Melbourne Cricket
Ground (MCG)**
If you cannot coincide
your visit with a sports
event at 'The G' it is
still worth a look.
Tours run on days
without events.
*Jolimont St.
Tel: (03) 9657 8879.
www.mcg.org.au.
Open: 9.30am–4.30pm;
tours 10am–3pm on days
without events. Admission
charge; tours extra.*

THE GREAT OCEAN ROAD TO ADELAIDE
Adelaide
ACCOMMODATION
**North Adelaide Heritage
Group ★★–★★★**
A wide array of heritage
properties dotted
around the city from
the unique Fire Engine
Suite to the cosy Café
Suite B&B.
*Tel: (08) 8272 1355.
www.adelaideheritage.
com*
Hotel Richmond ★★★
Quality contemporary
hotel in the city centre.
Also noted for its à la
carte restaurant.
*128 Rundell Mall.
Tel: (08) 8215 4444.
www.hotelrichmond.
com.au*
**Thorngrove
Manor ★★★★**
A member of the
prestigious Small
Luxury Hotels of
the World, this is a
Victorian Gothic Revival
building complete with
fantasy turrets and
towers. Sumptuous
rooms and suites all
adorned with period
antiques. Restaurant
complete with butler
service.

*2 Glenside Lane, Stirling.
Tel: (08) 8339 6748.
www.slh.com/thorngrove*

EATING OUT
**The Summit Restaurant
and Café ★★–★★★**
Situated on the edge
of the Adelaide Hills
and summit of 710m
(2329ft) Mount Lofty,
offering fine views across
the city. Both a café and
restaurant serving
Modern Australian
cuisine.
*Summit Rd, Mount Lofty.
Tel: (08) 8339 2600.
www.mtloftysummit.com.
Café open: Mon–Tue
9am–5pm, Wed–Sun
9am–late.
Restaurant open: lunch
noon–3pm, dinner
Wed–Sun from 6pm.*
**The Grange @
Hilton ★★★★**
Arguably the city's
best restaurant, and
home of celebrity chef
Cheong Liew, who has
since 1995 created
an imaginative fusion
of French and Asian
cuisine. Four different
degustation menus
are on offer, as well
as an à la carte three-
course meal.

233 Victoria Square.
Tel: (08) 8237 0737.
www.thegrangerestaurant.
com.au.
Open: Wed–Sat from
6.30pm.

ENTERTAINMENT
South Australian
Arts Centre
Best source of
information regarding
the city's theatrical and
sports events.
110 Hindley St.
Tel: (08) 8463 5444.
www.arts.sa.gov.au

SPORT AND LEISURE
Adelaide Oval
South Australia's
hallowed turf when
it comes to bat
and ball.
North Adelaide.
Tel: (08) 8300 3800.
www.cricketsa.com.au.
Tours: Mon–Fri on
non-match days only,
from 10am.

Apollo Bay to
Port Fairy
ACCOMMODATION AND
EATING OUT
Merrijig Inn ★★
Beautifully restored
and maintained 1841
homestead B&B.

Great-value
accommodation
consisting of four
charming ground-floor
suites and four small,
cosy attic rooms. The inn
also boasts an in-house
à la carte restaurant
and bar.
1 Campbell St,
Port Fairy.
Tel: (03) 5568 2324.
www.merrijiginn.com.
Open: daily to
non-guests for dinner
from 6pm, bookings
essential.
Cape Otway
Lighthouse Keepers'
Cottages ★★★–★★★★
Two options, either
the Head Keeper's
Cottage with kitchen,
lounge (open fire),
two bedrooms and
bathroom, or the
smaller studio-style
Assistant Keeper's
Cottage. Two nights'
stay minimum
recommended.
The Lightkeeper's
Café nearby offers
breakfast and lunch
(*Open: 9.30am–4.30pm*).
14km (7 miles) off the
Great Ocean Rd.
Tel: (03) 5237 9240.
www.lightstation.com

Kangaroo Island
ACCOMMODATION
Kangaroo Island
Wilderness
Resort ★★–★★★
Located at the southeast
corner, this all-in-one
retreat is a good mid-
range option. Eco-lodge
rooms and motel-style
suites with bath or spa.
Guest-only restaurant,
shop and petrol.
South Coast Rd (RSD 49),
Flinders Chase via
Kingscote.
Tel: (08) 8559 7275.
www.kiwr.com

Lorne to Apollo Bay
ACCOMMODATION AND
EATING OUT
Chris's Beacon Point
Restaurant and
Villas ★★★
Set in the Otway Ranges
overlooking the ocean,
this is a firm favourite
for both accommodation
and dining. Self-
contained luxury studio
or two-bedroom villa.
Quality à la carte dining,
with seafood and Greek
cuisine a speciality.
5km (3 miles) before
Apollo Bay. 280 Skenes
Creek Rd.
Tel: (03) 5237 6411.

www.chriss.com.au.
Open: daily 8–10am,
noon–2.30pm & 6–10pm.

Queenscliff
ACCOMMODATION AND
EATING OUT
Queenscliff Hotel ★★★
Classic Victorian
hotel built in 1887.
Traditional décor
throughout and
charming en-suite
rooms, some with
open fires. Quality
restaurant and bar.
Offers dinner.
16 Gellibrand St.
Tel: (03) 5258 1066.
www.queensclifffhotel.
com.au.
Open: Wed–Sat for dinner.

SPORT AND LEISURE
Go Ride a Wave
(Surfing)
Offers surfing lessons
in Torquay and
Anglesea.
143b Great Ocean Rd,
Anglesea; Shop 1,
15 Bell St, Torquay.
Tel: 1300 132 441.
www.gorideawave.com.au
The Torquay Surf
Academy
Surfing lessons in
Torquay.
34A Bell St, Torquay.

Tel: (03) 5261 2022.
www.torquaysurf.com.au

TASMANIA
Cradle Mountain and
Lake St Clair
ACCOMMODATION AND
EATING OUT
Cradle Mountain
Tourist Park ★★
This is the only option
for campervans and
tents. It is well facilitated
but overpriced. Simple,
self-contained cabins, a
large campsite, basic
alpine huts and a large,
warm kitchen. Bookings
essential in summer, even
for campsites.
Cradle Mountain.
Tel: (03) 6492 1395. www.
discoverholidayparks.
com.au
Derwent Bridge
Chalets ★★–★★★
Six self-contained
chalets, some with spa,
and cheaper studio
cabins located 5km
(3 miles) from the Lake
St Clair visitor centre.
Lyell Hwy.
Tel: (03) 6289 1000.
www.derwent-bridge.com
Cradle Mountain
Lodge ★★★★
Luxury cabins with
wood fires (but no TV,

phone or cooking)
dotted around a large,
wooden alpine lodge.
The lodge has open fires,
reading rooms, massage
and spa, sauna, bike hire,
guided walks and
nocturnal spotting tours.
Also has a restaurant,
bar and bistro open to
non-guests.
Cradle Mountain.
Tel: 1300 806 192/
(03) 6492 2103. www.
cradlemountainlodge.com.
au. Open: daily for
breakfast, lunch &
dinner.

Devonport
ACCOMMODATION
Hawley House ★★★
Set over 150ha
(371 acres) alongside
Hawley beach and
just a short drive
from Devonport, this
traditional homestead
and vineyard offers a
fine B&B option if you
are arriving by ferry.
Five immaculate
en-suites and loft rooms
in a former stable.
Dinner on request.
Hawley Beach, 22km/
14 miles from Devonport.
Tel: (03) 6428 6221.
www.hawleyhousetas.com

Franklin-Gordon Wild Rivers National Park

SPORT AND LEISURE

Rafting Tasmania

Owner Graham Mitchell was one of the first 50 people to raft the Franklin and has done more than 100 trips. The company now runs five-, seven- and ten-day trips from Nov–Apr for four to eight people. Experience of a lifetime.

Tel: (03) 6239 1080.
www.raftingtasmania.com

Freycinet National Park (Coles Bay)

ACCOMMODATION AND EATING OUT

Iluka Holiday Centre ★–★★★

The best bet for campervans or self-contained cabins and units. Shop, bar and restaurant nearby.

Coles Bay.
Tel: (03) 6257 0115.
www.ilukaholidaycentre.
com.au

Freycinet Lodge ★★★–★★★★

Luxury lodge and cabins beside Coles Bay and within the boundary of the national

park. Excellent facilities throughout including a formal and casual restaurant also open to non-guests. Organised activities include nocturnal wildlife walks.

Freycinet National Park.
Tel: (03) 6225 7000.
www.freycinetlodge.
com.au.
Open: daily for breakfast, lunch & dinner.

SPORT AND LEISURE

Freycinet Adventures

Extensive range of guided kayak trips from three hours to four days. Also independent kayak hire and a water-taxi service.

Coles Bay.
Tel: (03) 6257 0500. www.
freycinetadventures.com.au

Freycinet Air

Scenic flights over Wineglass Bay.

Friendly Beaches.
Tel: (03) 6375 1694.
www.freycinetair.com.au

Hobart

ACCOMMODATION

Colville Cottage ★★★

Hosted B&B in a historic Battery Point home with period furnishings such

as antique beds made of Tasmanian timbers, breakfast conservatory, distinguished guest living room and great hospitality.

32 Mona St,
Battery Point.
Tel: (03) 6223 6968.
www.colvillecottage.
com.au

Hotel Grand Chancellor ★★★

Modern chain hotel and one of the city's highest buildings, located in prime position overlooking the waterfront and convenient for the Central Business District.

1 Davey St.
Tel: (03) 6235 4535.
www.hgchobart.com.au

EATING OUT

Retro ★★

Set right in the heart of Salamanca, Retro is everything a café should be. Relaxed atmosphere, fine coffee, newspapers, people-watching and pavement tables.

Salamanca Pl.
Tel: (03) 6223 3073.
Open: 8am–5pm.

Mures ★★–★★★
In a prime position between Construction and Victoria Docks, this is something of a Hobart landmark and institution. The ground floor is a large fish-and-chip café and fresh fish shop, while the first floor is a significantly more refined seafood restaurant.
Tel: (03) 6231 1999.
www.mures.com.au.
Café open: 11am–9pm.
Restaurant open: noon–2.30pm & 6–9.30pm.
Cornelian Bay Boat House Restaurant ★★★
Set right on the beach overlooking Cornelian Bay. Modern, spacious dining room with a sophisticated yet relaxed atmosphere, making the best of the location. The fusion cuisine combines traditional French training with Asian flavours using fresh Tasmanian produce, and there are some vegetarian options. Good-value lunches. Live twilight jazz every Thursday and Friday night from 6–8pm.
Queens Walk, Cornelian Bay. Tel: (03) 6228 9289.

Open: daily for lunch from noon, Mon–Sat for dinner from 6.30pm.

ENTERTAINMENT
The Republic
The best bet for live music most nights of the week, normally blues or jazz. Relax on a cosy sofa around the wood fires.
Elizabeth St, North Hobart.
Tel: (03) 6234 6954.
Open: lunch Wed–Sun noon–2pm, dinner daily 6–10pm.
Theatre Royal
Australia's oldest theatre and the city's principal venue for major productions, theatre and musicals.
29 Campbell St.
Tel: (03) 6233 2299.
www.theatreroyal.com.au
Wrest Point Casino
Melbourne and Sydney may have the edge on size but not age – this was Australia's first casino, opened in 1973. The complex has four restaurants, including one that revolves, plus the Blackjacks Entertainment Venue.
2km (1¼ miles) south of the city centre just off Sandy Bay Rd, Wrest

Point. Tel: (03) 6225 0112.
www.wrestpoint.com.au.
Open: 11am–late.

SPORT AND LEISURE
Lady Nelson
Local cruises at weekends aboard the 1798 tall ship.
Elizabeth St Pier.
Tel: (03) 6234 3348.
www.ladynelson.org.au
Par-Avion
Offers a wide range of superb scenic flights (some with activity adjuncts) throughout the South and West (connections to Launceston and beyond).
Tel: (03) 6248 5390.
www.paravion.com.au

Launceston
ACCOMMODATION
Penny Royal Hotel and Apartments ★★–★★★
Large, characterful complex of modern suites and self-contained apartments in and around the former flour mill. Short stroll to the city or Cataract Gorge.
147 Paterson St.
Tel: (03) 6331 6699. www.leisureinnhotels.com.au
Werona ★★★–★★★★
Luxury boutique B&B set in a heritage (1908)

home with lovely views across the Tamar River Valley. Immaculate standard of accommodation and facilities, with a choice of period-furnished suites.
33 Trevallyn Rd.
Tel: (03) 6334 2272.
www.werona.com

EATING OUT
Stillwater ★★–★★★
Local favourite on the waterfront with the mellow timber floor and beams of the old mill. Asian-influenced creative cooking in the evening, and a breakfast and lunch café. Book ahead.
Ritchies Mill, 2 Bridge St.
Tel: (03) 6331 4153.
www.stillwater.net.au.
Open: breakfast & lunch until 4pm, dinner 6–9pm.

Port Arthur
ACCOMMODATION
Comfort Inn ★★
The closest accommodation to Port Arthur, with views over the ruins. En-suite motel rooms, mid-range restaurant.
Port Arthur Historic Site.
Tel: (03) 6250 2101.

www.portarthur-inn. com.au
Norfolk Bay Convict Station ★★–★★★
Former 1838 convict outpost in a peaceful waterside position 10km (6 miles) from Port Arthur, which can claim to be Australia's first railway station. Five en-suite B&B rooms.
Arthur Hwy. Taranna.
Tasman Peninsula.
Tel: (03) 6250 3487.
www.convictstation.com

Strahan
ACCOMMODATION
Risby Cove ★★–★★★
Former sawmill now housing chic one- or two-bedroom suites, an in-house café/restaurant and art gallery, all overlooking the waterfront.
The Esplanade.
Tel: (03) 6471 7572.
www.risby.com.au.
Restaurant open: 7am–8pm.
Renison Cottages ★★★
Four stylish, former miners' cottages in a quiet bush setting close to the town centre. Fully self-contained, open fires and bath/spas.
32–36 Harvey St.

Tel: (03) 6471 7390. www. renisoncottages.com.au

EATING OUT
Franklin Manor and Restaurant ★★★
Elegant boutique guesthouse and restaurant combined. Excellent rooms and apartments and the best fine dining option in town.
The Esplanade.
Tel: (03) 6471 7311. www. franklinmanor.com.au

SPORT AND LEISURE
4-Wheelers
A guided blast around the Henty Dunes on quad bikes.
Tel: (04) 1950 8175.
www.4wheelers.com.au
Strahan Seaplanes and Helicopters
Numerous options including the Gordon River tour.
Tel: (03) 6471 7718.
www.adventureflights. com.au
World Heritage Cruises
Well-established operator offering half-day cruises up the Gordon River.
The Esplanade.
Tel: (03) 6471 7174.
www.worldheritagecruises. com.au

Index

Acknowledgements

Thomas Cook Publishing wishes to thank REBECCA ROBINSON and DARROCH DONALD, to whom the copyright belongs, for the photographs in this book, except for the following images:

DREAMSTIME.COM 25 (Michal Steckiw)
FLICKR/eOn 48, Navin75 92, biguana 115, lin padgham 131
MARY EVANS PICTURE LIBRARY 113
WIKIMEDIA COMMONS/Astrokey44 112
WORLD PICTURES/PHOTOSHOT 125

For CAMBRIDGE PUBLISHING MANAGEMENT LTD:

Project editor: Karen Beaulah
Copy editor: Joanne Osborn
Typesetter: Paul Queripel
Proofreader: Jan McCann
Indexer: Karolin Thomas

SEND YOUR THOUGHTS TO
BOOKS@THOMASCOOK.COM

We're committed to providing the very best up-to-date information in our travel guides and constantly strive to make them as useful as they can be. You can help us to improve future editions by letting us have your feedback. If you've made a wonderful discovery on your travels that we don't already feature, if you'd like to inform us about recent changes to anything that we do include, or if you simply want to let us know your thoughts about this guidebook and how we can make it even better – we'd love to hear from you.

Send us ideas, discoveries and recommendations today and then look out for your valuable input in the next edition of this title.

Emails to the above address, or letters to the traveller guides Series Editor, Thomas Cook Publishing, PO Box 227, Coningsby Road, Peterborough PE3 8SB, UK.

Please don't forget to let us know which title your feedback refers to!